Firebird

"It is not so much Doty's experiences that elevate *Firebird*. It is the extraordinary lilt of his words, each chosen with great care, which makes even ordinary moments . . . become fresh and indelible."   —*Fort Lauderdale Sun Sentinel*

"The arrival of a great poet is magical. The world seems exhausted, nothing new is anticipated or deemed possible; suddenly, a new voice, new music, new wisdom, a new complex personality; the human is redefined and the exhausted world comes to life again, is alive with possibility. Mark Doty is a great poet, and *Firebird* describes how a great poet was formed. It is one of the most beautiful and moving testaments to the power of art I've read, and it's an exploration of the power and processes of memory as well—as the title suggests, this is a story of regeneration, or resurrection. It's as vivid, beautiful, endlessly delightful, and wonderfully, amazingly generous as his poems are. Here is a poet whose words are, in every sense, a benediction."

—Tony Kushner

"Mark Doty has written a memoir about his own childhood that is so perfectly remembered and beautifully described that it's both about one particular childhood, and all childhoods, happy or unhappy. *Firebird* captures childhood's solitariness, its occasional, almost farcical, faith in coming transformations, its abiding love of people and things. It's also a story that is heartbreaking and funny and thrilling and like nothing I've ever read before."   —Elizabeth McCracken,
author of *The Giant's House*

Firebird

A Memoir

MARK DOTY

Perennial

An Imprint of HarperCollins*Publishers*

Grateful acknowledgment is made to the following for permission to reprint lyrics from the songs "Downtown" and "Season of the Witch":

DOWNTOWN
Words and Music by Tony Hatch
Copyright © 1965, 1992 by Welbeck Music Canada, Universal Music Publishing Group, Inc.
Copyright renewed.
International Copyright Secured. Used by Permission. All Rights Reserved.

SEASON OF THE WITCH by Donovan Leitch
Copyright © 1966 by Donovan (Music) Ltd.
Administered by Peer International Corporation.
Copyright renewed.
International Copyright Secured. Used by Permission.

Page iv photograph courtesy of Mark Doty

A hardcover edition of this book was published in 1999 by HarperCollins Publishers.

HarperCollins books may be purchased for educational, business, or sales promotional use. For information please write: Special Markets Department, HarperCollins Publishers Inc., 10 East 53rd Street, New York, NY 10022.

First Perennial edition published 2000.

Designed by Elina D. Nudelman

The Library of Congress has catalogued the hardcover edition as follows:

Doty, Mark.
     Firebird : a memoir / Mark Doty. — 1st ed.
        p.   cm.
     ISBN 0-06-019374-3
     1. Doty, Mark—Childhood and youth. 2. Poets, American—20th century—Family relationships. 3. Memphis (Tenn.)—Social life and customs. 4. Poets, American—20th century—Biography. 5. Family—Tennessee—Memphis. 6. Doty, Mark—Family. I. Title.
PS3554.0798Z467   1999
811'.54—dc21
[B]   99-15619

ISBN 0-06-093197-3 (pbk.)

00 01 02 03 04 ❖/RRD 10 9 8 7 6 5 4 3 2 1

For Virginia Tynes
and for Rafael Campo

Where is your Self to be found? Always
in the deepest enchantment that you have
experienced.

Hugo von Hofmannsthal

Contents

Perspective Box

It seems a sort of peculiar toy at first, this elaborate painted box: a curiosity, almost ugly—what is this weird antique? I've been walking through room after room of paintings hung against the museum walls' deep silks, rainy afternoon light filtering down through the skylights above, galleries full of splendid things. But somehow it's this dim little side chamber—where a spotlight shines on this unwieldy object, right in the center—which I can't seem to leave.

Perspective Box with Views of a Dutch Interior was made in the middle years of the seventeenth century, in Antwerp or Amsterdam, by one Samuel Von Hoogstraten, Dutch painter, aficionado of perspective, connoisseur of the complicated effects of light. A man who loved the eye's involvement in the world. A man who lied with pigment; painting, he wrote, "deceives in a permissible, pleasurable, and praiseworthy manner."

I've been thinking about praise, and the praiseworthy, all day—or rather, trying *not* to think about them. I'm entirely, irremediably nervous. I've come to London because I am among the finalists for a literary award, meeting British poets and publishers, doing some interviews with the press and BBC radio. The event's surrounded by a hoopla no American poetry award would ever generate; the *Independent*, reporting on the reading last night, where each finalist read a poem or two, described me as "a whispery beanpole." I am behaving as though I am a calm and more-or-less balanced adult, but in fact I'm reduced to something distinctly adolescent by the whole thing. Of course I'd like to win the prize, but can't quite let myself imagine that; I don't like to imagine the alternative either. Both options make my self-doubt flare, since to win would seem the strangest of flukes, an honor I couldn't possibly merit, and to lose would confirm my own restless doubts. This is the terrible dilemma of prizes: we cannot believe we deserve them, and we cannot quite believe we don't.

I am a believer in self-doubt, in my better moments; there's nothing like an appropriate amount of it to keep us humane, clear-headed, level. But under these circumstances I have no perspective on my doubts, which seem to be mounting and vibrating, slapping against me like the waves I stirred up this morning, swimming furious laps in a public pool in Soho.

Wandering the National Gallery's cool and formal chambers, I am trying to get as far from myself and my anticipation of the evening as I can get, and perhaps that's what this strange wooden contraption promises.

I learn from the label on the wall that there are six of these *perspectyfkas*, as they were called in Dutch, remaining in the world, flowers of a minor artistic tradition. In the fifteenth century, Italian artists enthralled with perspective constructed boxes to experiment with the illusion of depth; their projects exemplified the passionate Renaissance marriage of science and art, their love for the mathematics of vision. French and German painters made "peep shows," shadowbox assemblages of wax figures and objects, theaters behind glass. But the Dutch perspective boxes contained nothing at all, nothing but paint.

This one's perched on an elaborate black stand, and embel-

lished on its top and sides with decorative motifs: cherubs, imple-
ments of the artist's work. One wall of the box has been left open,
covered now with a sheet of Lucite, so that I can peer into the inte-
rior: painted walls and floor and ceiling, all representing the inte-
rior of a room. Uncurtained windows, open doors, furniture and
books, paintings and mirrors, coats hung on a wall rack, a letter
dropped on the floor's geometric tiles: ordinary life.

But something's strangely wrong. Some things are too large,
others tiny, and nearly all seem bent or misshapen, twisted
weirdly around corners or across floors and walls. That shape on
the floor? A spaniel, his four paws resting firmly on the ground,
but above his legs his body stretches wildly up the wall as though
he'd been caught in a carnival mirror. The dizzy pattern of the
floor tiles spins, as if in the vertigo of the world's worst case of
astigmatism. This is serenity transmogrified, Vermeer on hallu-
cinogens.

But in the two walls which abut the transparent side are peep-
holes, little lenses like the eyepieces of telescopes. And when I
place my eye to those disks of glass—revelation! The painted room
suddenly *is* a room, each thing in place and in perspective. I can
see every key on the virginal, the sharp outlines of the dropped let-
ter (addressed to Von Hoogstraten himself, is this his house?), the
boots and jacket in their place, the good dog who has been waiting
to be seen.

The painter has rendered distortion so exactly that the lens cor-
rects it perfectly; he paints the world misshapen, and the glass
shapes it right again. Which means that he has had to *mis*shape
things just so, to bend forms so that light through the lens will
bend them back again.

Why in the world go to this much trouble? Samuel Von
Hoogstraten's compatriots went to astonishing lengths to capture
light transfixing a slice of lemon peel, the touch of sun on the lip
of a pewter pitcher. All that struggle to get things right, and then he
takes evident pleasure in painstakingly getting them *wrong*. Or at
least seeming to, until the correcting lens reveals to us that his
chaos is, in fact, art.

I try to walk away, but find myself stopping at the door, turn-
ing, walking the perimeter of the little room to view the box from

all sides. Then I'm pulled back to it again, unsatisfied, wanting more.

The room where nothing's clear, even the dog smeared up the side of the wall—that room comes clear, seen through the right glass. The lens corrects, clarifies, puts things in their proper arrangement. The glass lozenge allows me to see that I am looking into not merely one room but a house: there are chambers beyond this one, rooms with people in them—a woman reading, quietly, in a chair beside a window's wash of cool Northern light. That Dutch glow seems made of both physical light and the lamp-shine of interiority, the polish things acquire in the steady, affectionate illumination of attention. Occupied rooms, lit by our seeing.

He doesn't believe in darkness, Samuel Von Hoogstraten, doesn't hold with chiaroscuro; for him clarity is all, and isn't it possible that clarity might shine into every corner of the house, might bring its resolving certainty to everything, bring each object into right relation with all the other things in this little world: his terrarium, his terrestrial comedy of illusion? Does he mean that even the most distorted form might come true? No matter how deep the trouble, how twisted the form, the rectifying lens of art could set it right?

Or no—does he mean it this way, that art *must* distort, must bend the shapes of things? If this hellish playhouse weren't deranged, then the device wouldn't work, the lens would smear rather than resolve, cripple these figures rather than bring them to life.

But there are *two* lenses, dual peepholes through which to peer into this little chamber. Is that the point? Always a choice to make, which aperture to put the eye to. From either direction the house goes on and on, and even at the end of the diminishing series of chambers there isn't an end but a doubt—a slice of room, maybe another door, at least a window that bathes a woman or a man who can't be seen, a map or a Turkey carpet, in that pearly winter light. Perhaps a mirror's hung on the wall, and in that way the chain of rooms *is* infinite, continuous, unknowable.

I try again to move on, into the next, brighter gallery. But it's no use, it's Samuel Von Hoogstraten I'm thinking of. What I want to be is alone, in this intimate room, with his box. When anyone else enters I wait in a corner till the intruder passes on, until I can return to my private study.

Maybe he was driven by doubt, too, unable to rest in two dimensions? His rooms and hallways have the almost-depth of stereopticon views, or those 3-D contraptions of my childhood, View-Masters, a sort of plastic binocular in which spun a cardboard disc holding transparent slides; pull the trigger, the disc turned, and the slides told a little story: wonders of the Grand Canyon, the labors of Hercules, the sorrows of Bambi.

What did Von Hoogstraten think he was doing? Who knows what he believed? What's important is the resonant object, here, now, inviting interpretation and resisting it at once, a physical embodiment not of one idea but of many. It breathes with that odd, cold, long life that some works of art have.

This motionless thing—which has long outlived its moment of fashionable novelty, its unrecapturable context—offers a permanent demonstration, in its deep silence. Here is chaos brought to order and order dissolving again. We think that art makes order out of the unruly, but here chaos is made, too. And so we're allowed to play, serious children, in Von Hoogstraten's dialectic: back and forth, between the formless and the formed, worlds of appearance. Disorder resolves into pattern, then dissolves again, back and forth, as long as I stay.

Which might be all afternoon; I have all day, nowhere to be till evening. I don't know that in a few hours T. S. Eliot's widow—charming, a bit vague around the edges, a blond blur—will present to my book a prize named for her late husband, and that she and I and my British editor and various luminaries will all head off for a celebratory dinner in some fancy London *boîte*, where she'll tell me stories of her life with "Tom" thirty years before. (My favorite: driving through Cape Cod, they tossed martinis out the window, with the intention of intoxicating the squirrels.)

The pressure of the competition seems a world away; I've lost myself in the world of this box. And I feel at home here, strangely, though I'm thousands of miles from anything I know; there's something familiar about this house, something oddly comforting and unsettling at once, hard to resist.

And suddenly I want to lift off the lid of the box, want to break all the rules and grab hold of it, rip off the roof so I can peer down into those rooms. . . . Though it wouldn't work even if I could do it; there's no choice but to look through a lens.

Maybe around some corner—at some angle I'll finally discover, if I lean into the eyepiece, if my eye works hard enough to probe the hidden recesses—I'll find them, not Samuel Von Hoogstraten's hidden people but my own, the family I can't seem to see through any more direct means. They are hard to approach; they don't want to be known.

Memory confounds and veils them, and were they ever clear to begin with? They were hidden from each other by a distorting rage, by sorrow, by the plain nameless gulf that comes between people. Whatever became of their kindness? Hard to see them even now, years later, far away from them, years away. Can I find them in these phantom rooms (only paint, only light on a screen) whose entrances and exits bend and shadow, diminish and vanish?

I look deeper into the dreamed house: sonorous old clock marking the shadowy hour. Sad objects: ancient blue pitcher with a stag in high relief, cracked blue-and-white cups, photographs of the dead, faces cooling as they travel on into their seclusion. Who knows their names now? Sway of the old clock's golden pendulum. Sepia print of hunting dogs pointing to unseen prey. Glasses chill with gleaming distillates: vodka, turpentine. And here is the woman, weeping beside a painting she's made, a bruised-looking bowl of lilacs, their cloud of dark panicles seething anger or sorrow. If I came upon her when she didn't expect anyone, mightn't I see something that would help me to understand her, and the obliterating gesture she'll make toward her son?

The museum vanishes.

Cool black pistol dreaming in a drawer. A folding wooden yardstick edged in brass, precise case of drafting tools, a man also seething: resentment, loneliness? Though he's well hidden, attempting to disappear in my dollhouse mirrors. A lace-paper doily folded into a little fan, a souvenir: here the daughter who's already gone, smart girl, run as far and fast as she can. In this room—so far back in the house you wonder that you could ever find him!—a boy lost in a book, which is itself a tiny box. He's dreaming into its unseen rooms, rooms he'll travel all his life. Somewhere in the air above him a strange bird flashes by, flutter and hurry, bright turbulence. The book he's reading configures this space: house and mother, sister and closet and father, endless hallway, tumult of wings. His book angles and skews them by artifice, and then tries to use artifice to set them right.

PART ONE

Rainbow Girls

In 1959, in Memphis, Tennessee, my sister, Sally, became a Rainbow Girl. She'd been initiated, she told me, into a secret society. What did it mean? What were they not allowed to tell? It was my family's year for the sororal; my mother joined the Order of the Eastern Star and wore around her neck a little golden symbol which indicated her membership. I liked their name—ceremonial, vaguely Egyptian—but the simple necklace was far less interesting than the florid ephemera of the Rainbow Girls, the things Sally hid in the treasury of her lowest dresser drawer, mementos of every one of their occasions.

I am not allowed in her room, but I adore secrets, or rather secrecy's trappings, especially the hidden souvenirs of my sister's beauty, her unseen evenings.

Memory (stage designer, costumer, expert in theatrical lighting) orchestrates the scene like this: my sister's darkened room, a little summer twilight bluing the window and the chest of drawers. *Chif-ferobe*, my grandmother calls it, rich old word that seems itself to smell like a closed drawer; *bureau*, my father says, polished word, waxy, tobacco colored. This one isn't dark and varnished like my grandparents' stuff, or the hodgepodge of old furniture in the other houses we've lived in; this new blond suite, angular, forward looking, seems a physical expression of my sister's grownupness and privacy. My parents never buy anything new, so who knows where it's come from; they must have had some little flourish of money as well as some burst of interest in style. Or did Sally choose it? She is almost sixteen, I am newly six; she will leave home soon, but we don't know that yet. For now the important thing for me is that she has become a Rainbow Girl. Is that where she is tonight, off with her new sisters? My parents are down the hall in the living room, watching television, far away, absorbed in something that does not concern me, so I am free to pursue my investigations.

Her room is full of things that might invite my attention: a luscious satin pillow a boyfriend won for her at a fair, with verses written on it in stiff gold cursive and a border of irresistible yellow fringe. An autograph hound, a stuffed dachshund with a lean body of white cloth on which her friends have written salutations and verses and names. A record case made just for 45s, an object that seems feminine and precise, exactly suited to its purpose: beige vinyl fabric, fabric hinges, and when you lift the lid her favorites are revealed, black and glossy. I could pull out the matching phonograph and plug it in, but that wouldn't really interest me much. I like to hear the openings of the songs she likes—"You Ain't Nothin' But a Hound Dog," "Love Me Tender," something by Brenda Lee—but I don't feel like sitting still for the rest of the song; I don't believe I will be rewarded for sustained attention. As I will be, I know with all my heart, the full certainty of my six-year-old power of belief, when I look into the drawer.

To recollect: that verb's exact, since here in the haze are elements of a collection, an assemblage of things so long unseen they might as well be the stuff of someone else's life. That fringed carnival pillow: I haven't seen that for forty years! And there it is, in sharp focus, weirdly noisy, the fabric crunching slightly when leaned into, its texture unpleasant but also fascinating, as you run a finger across the roughish print of the text and the satin interstices: scribble of a sentimental poem of devotion. And though the devoted and the devotee have long moved on, and the physical pillow vanished decades ago, its texture is precisely available to my fingertips now. Am I a repository of vanished things which float to the surface, slowly, one at a time, each with invisible links to another?

My raggedy stuffed tiger, for instance, with its green glass eyes—little fragments of the divine fire, alert, energetic, like something out of Blake, though of course I don't think that then. He has long been put away, in the attic of our house on Ramses Street (the front porch has wide columns which taper at the top, a watered-down reference to Luxor). On some excursion with my mother into that hot, sequestered place, reached only by a mysterious collapsing stair that folds down from the ceiling, I've found him again and have taken pleasure in the recognition, a pleasure more complicated than mere affection. The nicely battered tiger is of a time which I think of as the past—of, as it were, childhood's childhood. Now, at six, I have a past; I have an object which refers to who I used to be.

But the drawer, precious and hermetic, refers to who I am now. And to something else, something veiled, and perhaps there's even a veil inside it, among these scraps of sheer and sparkled treasure. Sally must have shown them to me, proud of her new sense of belonging, though what they meant to her and what they mean to me are quite different things. For her they're evidence of a common bond, proof of sisterhood; for me they are alluring artifacts of difference.

On my knees in the half dark, I slip the drawer open, and it's like a pirate chest opened in a movie, little glimmers brilliant on the faceted surfaces of the treasures, little musical chimes sounding as if these were audible jewels. No light in the room except the glow emanating from these things, which include: a fan made from stiff folded net fabric—did Sally call it chiffon? No, that was the filmy beige stuff on her prom dress; this is tulle, striped, one watery hue merging into another, a skyey spectrum like the prisms in the air in my ViewMaster slides of Niagara Falls, rainbows over a lucky boat named *Maid of the Mist*. Glittery ribbons, carnations made from Kleenex clipped with a bobby pin and fringed, just so, then unfolded into a burst of imitation blossom, one drop of cologne fragrant at the center. Scents, powders, delicious nail colors, an album into which she's pressed Rainbow invitations: the night all the new girls dressed as pickaninnies, required to do their faces from this round tin of blackface. They put their hair in one hundred—count them—little pigtails. Better: the invitation to the Rainbow Cotillion, inside whose stiff engraved fold of paper floats a perfect bit of aurora, like a ripple of colored atmosphere. *Aurora*: undulation of three vowels moving like heat-shimmer up off the Memphis pavement. *Cotillion*: I fall into the warm haze of the word, which contains crepe-paper flowers pinned to wrists and sashes, arbors made from twisted bits of tissue paper, and somewhere there are bells, reverberant as though the cotillion were held underwater, and bell-shaped dresses—tulle and chiffon and the stiff gold-printed satin of the pillow, the lovely whiplike tentacles of the fringe—all circling forever, almost untouchable, in a sphere of their own. In the album are ticket stubs and place cards and flattened decorated nut cups, party favors, beside which the familiar daily world of our house and things, the plain navy and dull scarred brown of my school seem dun, workaday—unseasoned, a tired old broth redolent of nothing but necessity.

Something about this pleasure feels entirely private. How do I know this is something to hide? Partly it's just that this room and its thrilling stuff are *hers*, but something runs deeper than that: my fetishism isn't about Sally but about beauty itself, about wrappings and presentation and display, about artifice and its perfection.

∽

My education in beauty had already begun, and the new experience of school brought its brightest exemplar. Little Miss Sunbeam—whose face emblazoned an infinity of bread wrappers, whose image glowed on the sides of fleets of bakery trucks, the buttered bread in her hands like some physical manifestation of happiness—came to Peabody Elementary for purposes of entertainment, as if we were troops who required some recreational distraction, and for the rather shameless promotion of cottony white bread. (Our own brand of bread is Rainbo. I like to steal slices from the kitchen, put the slices in a Mason jar with the lid screwed on tight, and bury it in the backyard. When I dig it up, magic: little galaxies of blue-black mold, *fleurs du mal*.) Some message about achievement must also have been implied in our grade-school assembly, since this perfect child was so accomplished she merited elevation to the fierce light of our auditorium's stage.

Peabody was a square building, imposing, multistoried, of gray and somnolent cement, something of civic pride or cultural ambition about it, something already historical and over by the time I got there, though no one had really noticed yet. A Gilbert Stuart portrait of George Washington hung in our classroom. It was unfinished, my teacher said, which is why his shoulders rose out of nothing, a billow of blank canvas, though it looked to me as if the Father of Our Country poked his head up through a bank of summer clouds, though he seemed oblivious to them, cheerlessly and permanently important. We faced him and the flag first thing in the morning to say the Pledge of Allegiance, sing a verse of "My Country 'Tis of Thee," and then sit down at our desks, bow our heads, and mumble some unmemorable prayer. The best part of the song was the lines

> From ev'ry mountainside
> Leh-et freedom ring

which offered a deliciously abstract, vague prospect to visualize, something you could think about but not see. Lessons all day, mostly involving letters, phonics; I loved the phrase "consonant blend" and liked to say it to myself. White chalk dust, foggy clouds of it, when the erasers are taken outside and beaten out. Milk money, and the worn white marble stairs going up, up into Peabody School to the library, when we're taken there for a story, lined up according to our height. I am the tallest boy in first grade, but I don't feel large. I am a very careful boy. I want to do well and am aware of certain dangers. Take my Dick and Jane book, that reader in which little bouquets of short declarative sentences so quickly replace the new magic of deciphering the code with the boring actuality of what the symbols represent: "See Puff eat." We are each assigned a copy of the book, which we keep in our desks and are sometimes allowed to take home. I look ahead, curious about what else might appear on the stiff, strange-smelling pages, and right in the middle of my book is a horror: a starburst of mold, somebody's old—jelly sandwich maybe?—smashed right between father (in his brown fedora, just like my father's) and Dick and Spot. Not cool and beautiful like my buried bread-mold garden but too vivid, fierce. I am scared my teacher will think I've done this, violated the book; I'm responsible for it, after all, and I love my book even if it is weirdly boring and we read it so slowly, as if we are savoring something as insubstantial as a slice of that airy bread. I want to hide it, but the smell is so disgusting I have to tell her, and she doesn't blame me at all.

I can tell she *does* blame a girl named Valerie, though, who one day defecates on the floor while we are sitting at our desks working. How does she do it? She has her underpants on and a dress, a plaid wool jumper in a red-and-yellow tartan that suddenly looks sad, and yet right there on the linoleum only a desk or two in front of mine are two little turds, firm, perfectly formed, and terrifying. Many of us know the poop has come into the room with us before the teacher does, and when she discovers it other things seem forgotten. The big printed letters that ring the room, each lowercase version beside its capital parent, the clumsy tablets with alternating solid and broken blue lines, to help us shape the letters we practice with our fat pencils—all are eclipsed by the poop. Teacher picks it up with tissues. I'm aware of her red fingernails, a faint sweet scent of talcum. She doesn't shout or spank Valerie, but somehow it's worse. She says, "Why didn't you ask to go to the bathroom?" Valerie doesn't answer. Of course there isn't any answer, so Valerie looks all the smaller in her hapless Scotch plaid and I take it all in; I don't ever want to ask to go the bathroom (marble, cool, noise of water, big boys), because somehow I wouldn't want anyone to know I need to, but this means you have to choose between two kinds of shame, and Valerie made a bad choice.

A danger: out on the asphalt playground, from which the school's flung up into the air vertical as a Venetian palace, is a shady corner where immense old trees have been allowed to stay. The huge circumference of one oak (treasure of fallen acorns, in September) borders the street, half on the playground, half buck-

16

∾

M
a
r
k

D
o
t
y

ling the sidewalk in a slow and undramatic earthquake. On this sidewalk, somebody said, a man in a car offered a girl candy. *Come into my car with me, and I will give you candy.* Then what happened? Something to do with safety.

I walk home from school on streets with big trees, sometimes wet in the rain, which brings new pleasures: dark navy and black umbrellas, unfurling vinyly smell. Safety patrols in their yellow slickers. Safety patrols! Another danger: big kids with shiny plastic sashes and authority with which they probably shouldn't have been entrusted. They have their own cloakroom, a clubhouse repository for their uniforms, and five minutes before school is over for everyone else a special bell rings and the safety patrols hurry to their cloakroom, don their badges and sashes, and rush to their corners. I have been to their room, once, on Halloween, when there was a special showing of *The Creature from the Black Lagoon.* The cloakroom itself seemed permanently moist, full of slick things, swathed in darkness.

The yellow-harnessed safety patrols came to seem scarier to me after the safety movie. The entire school was assembled; we first-graders marched into the auditorium last while the older kids watched us. Big numbers and visual static fired on the huge screen, large as the stage itself, pulled down over the red velvet curtain.

The movie concerned terrible things which happen to children who aren't careful. One girl walked home from school every day along a path that required her to go around a train yard, but that way was long and not as interesting as the parked trains, so the girl decided to take a shortcut, which means she broke a rule I didn't know: Never Walk Under a Parked Train. I've never been on or near a train, but still it's something I don't know. How many rules don't I know? The girl walks under the train, it's dark under there, there's a rumble and then everything swirls around into sirens and there she is in a hospital, bandaged and covered with cuts and dark shapes as if the dark under the train got on her skin, a tube in her nose, and bags of blood hang in the air next to her bed and maybe she won't live. Some children won't live, not if they're not safe. Don't Cross the Street without Looking, Don't Take Candy from Men: the movie's horrible and the horror's thrilling, too. The movie makes you think your body is vulnerable, subject to invasion, cutting apart; that means you *have* a body, *are* a body. Like the moldy pages in my reader, the movie's shocking, physical. Seeing blood is like seeing Valerie's poop: it comes from inside you, can't always be held in, makes trouble, makes everything shriek and stop. Walking home from school: step, step, my legs, step, swing, my arms, look, swivel, wish, my head. Soul way down in there, little winged me, little shoot, like when you cut open an onion and there's that new green hidden in the center, wanting to shout its way out, but be careful: lose your body and the soul jumps out, like the little man my grandmother told me jumps out of the log in the fire when you hear that pop—that sound means he's broken free of the wood that held him. But you don't want to break free, do you? Body feels strange, alien when you stand back from it: rub the back of your neck, just where the hair starts: whose hair, whose head?

Our auditorium was put to less sanguine but equally instructive use the day Little Miss Sunbeam appeared. Was the girl on the bread wrapper actually drawn in her likeness? More likely I saw one of a series of Misses, since all that was required were apple cheeks, a pinafore, and those signifying ringlets, weirdly quaint and otherworldly even in 1959. Who was she? Older than as presented, I imagine, a girlish almost-teen in a Shirley Temple dress, white ankle socks, and tap-shoe Mary Janes.

Those tap shoes! They partook of something, gleamed with that Rainbow Girl allure—something like a kind of ectoplasm spread across an ordinary surface, transformative, lending the lucky thing a resonance, an authority.

Silence, the house lights dimming, the velvet curtain black now, and drawn. A drumroll, and then a voice we've never heard before, an assured voice from TV or the circus, "Ladies and gentlemen, boys and girls, brought to you by the Sunbeam Bread Company, the little lady herself, Little Miss Sunbeam!"

And she launches herself through the curtain's opening, flinging both sides back with a showgirl's knowing toss of the arms, and begins to dance a full-throttle no-holds-barred tap routine. She is a dynamic entity of blondness, legs, and polka dots, her arms spun in circles as she does time steps, tap shoes clicking out an entrancing speedy patter, ringlets bouncing, and then—wonder—

she opens her mouth to sing, and does. *What* I could not tell you now, can in fact barely reconstruct the details of her performance, it is such a rhapsodic blur of aesthetic achievement, show business, and glamour. Her dance seems spontaneous, so effortless does she make each move appear, but of course it's carefully planned, a faultlessly executed performance of who she's labored so to become, any sign of her work subsumed in the bravura of her art. She is my first diva, probably all of twelve, a painted doll in rouge and big eyelashes, and who wouldn't be entranced by such a production? Since it's both transcendent and a little frightening at once: she is of us and yet so much more than us; there is no danger to *her* body; she is beyond limit and has entered a realm in which she is above all harm.

∾

I have a problem with my parents, which has to do with what to call them. I don't know when this began, the origins of my situation seem to go so deeply into the past. I've only six years of experience, far less of memory, but as my tiger demonstrates, forgetting is a long, deep well, already dark with layers of unrecorded time. Who knows what occasions and relics that seemingly empty shaft contains? I have no conscious awareness of this problem, of course, as children never have terms for what in their lives is truly grave.

With each parent, this difficulty arises from opposite causes. My relationship with my mother is immense to me, and occupies so much space I can barely see around it. She is both my element and also somehow singular, slightly forbidding; she is not to be displeased. Though she is often quite tender to me, there is something about her which precludes ease; that's the signal characteristic of our relation: intimacy without ease. "Mom" seems out of the question, its casual, everyday quality entirely wrong; there is some gravity or strain to our connection which prohibits it. A good boy, I am in some way her representative in the world of better possibilities than she has known; I am to do well in school, am somehow precious. Things are expected of me, and such a child would address his mother *as* "Mother"—but that feels weirdly stiff because it acknowledges an absence of spontaneity: the term makes us part of a drama, makes me an actor in a family play.

With my father it's simpler: we simply lack connection. He's a force on the horizon, but a distant one, like the sort of storm you see in the Midwest, visible across uncountable acres of cornfields. Maybe it will sweep in to give you trouble but probably not, not often. In my mind he is concerned with a particular universe of things that have to do with his work: shiny metal lunch box, domed like a vaulted chapel. Drafting tools set precisely in leather cases, three-sided rulers for measuring what? Shiny white hard hat. Little red castle, two-towered, on a decal on the windshield of his government truck, emblem of the Army Engineers. Mornings he eats shredded wheat soaked in milk from a tall drinking glass while the coffee percolates, then he's gone. Home at night, home from a trip, sometimes he brings me something, some breakable little toy, reward for his absence. I manipulate him with expectation, make it clear that I will be so pleased to receive something (a "play-pretty," our term for toy, something I used to say as a baby) as consolation, but I already know I don't need consoling. After-shave, boxer shorts, milk of magnesia in blue bottles: mostly I don't need to call him anything.

Though just now I do, because I have done something wrong, and there is about to be a crisis, and only I can avert it.

I am in Sally's room, absorbed in the pleasures of the drawer. Above the bureau is a large mirror, and I am lifting things from the drawer up to see them in the glass, to see them beside my face: *real* play-pretties, though these aren't toys but instances, embodiments of beauty, and I am attempting some physical connection to them, seeking some relation between them and my body: what might be done with this, and this? How would one hold oneself, how compose the face, the look, to bring oneself into the realm of the things? Somehow the requirement is to bring the body into their universe, align it with their laws: how to become worthy of that shine? Here on the bureau top's a water glass, its base cut with little faceted grooves. I remember that to have perfect posture—Sally's told me this—you must learn to walk with something balanced on your head, a book or a drinking glass, and if you hold yourself perfectly erect and walk without the object falling from your head then you are a *model*. Meaning: different body, accomplishment of the body? I put the glass on top of my head, pulling myself up straight, the glass wobbles, I lift my arms up for balance, that's better, I'm getting it now. Another wobble, so I try moving my head from side to side a little like a Balinese dancer, and that's it, slip and disaster, the glass crashes to the floor and shatters, unnaturally loud.

Now we're in a movie again, a safety movie, in slow motion: I am standing paralyzed by what I've done, there's a rush and roar from the direction of the living room, my father rising from the couch, he's coming down the hall, I'm afraid he's going to spank me, I remember the last time, the humiliation of it, him pulling my pants down on the porch and whaling me, his red face filled up with blood and rage, striking at me because what have I done? *Now* I've done something plain and sharply lit like the big shards of glass on the floor, and I've backed up into the corner of the room, away from the breakage and away from the door he's about to come through, and as he does the movie gets even slower. He's a blur in pajama bottoms and white strap undershirt. He's running, one leg raised high in the air, high as my head, he's saying something, but the film's going so slow I can't understand it, something like, "What the hell have you done?" but the word *What* hangs in the air, oily, dark, and long. And I see that he's barefoot: his feet and ankles are pink and white, those are the colors of him, milky rosewater skin exposed beneath the blue pajama trousers, his foot's in the air and he's moving forward, he wants to see what I have broken and is about to step down hard in front of the bureau where the glass is, the biggest piece gleaming there with a diamond drop of light on its sharpest point like the glitter on the rainbow treasure gone cold and perverse.

I want to say, *Stop*, I want to say, *There's glass there, don't!* I have all the time in the world, as the film goes sputtering in the loops and sprockets of the old elementary school projector; I have minutes to say, *Daddy, don't step on the glass*. But nothing comes out of my mouth; I'm fixed there, forever, a boy who tried to be a model.

And then he screams. End of film, crackle, sputter, and then slap of the last bit of celluloid against the reel: somebody turn it off.

Now, here's my father on the couch, foot in a bowl of water my mother's brought, a big tin basin. Strangely I am not being punished, not even yelled at; I seem to have disappeared, my mother and father entirely occupied with the wound. The water in the basin turns pink, then deepens, a bowl of hellish rosé, and a pale piece of skin floats on the surface: pink and white.

I'm sent to what my parents call "the neighbor lady's" while they leave for the emergency room. There is some sense about this that I am being consoled, though of course I am not the wounded one; am I looking stricken, is my fear in my face? The neighbor lady has a wonderful maid named Martha; her lap's practically a continent. We sit at the kitchen table, me and the neighbor lady's daughter, whom Martha will only refer to as Miss Carla, although she is at most a fourth-grader. Martha makes popcorn for me in a black iron pot (cheery zing and pop against the lid) and says, "Child, your daddy's going to be all right."

∿

At all of eight or nine, Miss Carla requires a prefix of respect, her four-letter pedestal. She's acquired a certain hauteur; she is elongated—because she practices ballet daily, up on toes, hands above her head, becoming taller, more attenuated?—and a little cruel. She teaches me to burn ants on the sidewalk with a magnifying glass. I don't like it, don't see the point, except for the fascination of the circle of focused sunlight, its wavery edge becoming solid as it shrinks down to a punishing pinpoint, as Carla's very white hand finds just the right position for the lens. She incinerates them with abandon, and they writhe just an instant and wrinkle up. She catches lightning bugs in mayonnaise jars and carries the dying little lamps around as a kind of sorry torch. When I try this one evening, my mother says, "But they might be parents. What if their children are waiting for them?" and I let all the bugs go. Digging in the damp clay of the backyard, Carla and I find a perfectly enormous worm, a foot long and just as pink and big around as my thumb; with her toy spade she chops it in half with abandon, so that each half will grow a new body. She adores and cultivates her power and seeks new theaters of operation in which to exercise it. One day I am myself, in some subtle way not without its fascination, not without desire, its object. She opens her closet to show me her trove of ballet costumes: an arsenal, a ritual wardrobe, the treasure of the trolls kept in the dark beneath their bridge. Glitter and sequin and tulle upon tulle in layers, no single piece standing alone but each a part of an ensemble, each bodice with its attached tutu accompanied by headpieces and matching shoes, sleek and sheened, with their strange, blunt toes.

A show begins: Carla goes behind a door, emerges, in a bit, in the outfit of the moment, which is linked to a piece of music, which is linked to particular steps. The item revealed, coming to life as her body occupies it and steps into a position, then another. Then the scene's over, back behind the door, another outfit, soon the pieces strewn everywhere. Martha out in the hallway: "Miss Carla, are you in those clothes? You know your mother wants you to take good care of those." No response from Carla except that she goes to draw another suite of fabrics from the dark; Martha moves away, mumbling.

Why does it seem cruel? The show's somehow about titillation—not sexual, exactly, but a display of wealth and of possession. It demonstrates, for Carla, her power over the adults who've bought her this dragon hoard of glitter. For me her impromptu pageant is about the oddly potent associations of the stuff, and how she's transformed by it. Does she recognize in me some fascination or longing, a puzzled rapture in what she possesses? I sit on the edge of her bed, in thrall, powerless. The show continues, the *chef d'oeuvre* an extravaganza à la Josephine Baker: Carla emerges as a night sky, her black outfit the empyrean between the little lights of heaven. Bits of glimmer comprise a shifting disorder of constellations. Stiff black feathered cloche, black sequins, *noir* sparkle that rustles with a faint iridescence, prismatic gleam emerging from a rhapsody of gloom; Queen of the Night, Mistress of Devils, body of the Snow Queen, so milky she looks blue, especially in her shadowed armpits, the hollows of her legs as she spins then bolts across the room in near jetés, so long, angular, and black that she's a black swan, her long neck strained and undulant. No, better: a black flamingo.

Martha also looks blue, but because she is so black. I love her. She smells like clean ironed cotton, mostly because, when she comes to our house one day a week, or every other week, she spends the day ironing. My mother hates to iron, she says; on *her* ironing days, this ritual: she stands over the unfolded metal board with a big basket of clean laundry on the floor beside her: sheets, shirts, my father's patterned boxer shorts. On the edge of the board is her spray starch, a big ashtray, her flip-top box of Salems a deep mint green. Iron, smoke, spray the little atomized droplets, smoke, walk around, and smoke a little more. The gradual emptying of the basket seems endless, Sisyphean. One day when she's gone out I take one of the Salems for myself, light it, go out to the front porch and inhale the mentholed cloud, and am quickly dizzy and sick, swirling in my head like the girl who got hit by the train. Martha's ironing days are long and steady, no cigarettes; lovely scent of the hot iron and the smoothed clothes. A fine day for me, when Martha comes; I bring books or drawing paper and crayons and sprawl on the floor close to the ironing board, or pursue my favorite project of the moment, which is to cut magazine pages into very tiny triangles until I have filled a saucepan from the kitchen with them, and then I stir the paper with a spoon. Martha talks some about this and that: the weather, the work I am doing, her children. One day I meet them, when she brings them to Carla's house for a visit, because there's some problem and Martha doesn't have anyplace else for them to go that afternoon, which they must spend playing outside while she works; three small girls in clean, worn dresses, their faces scrubbed to shining, hair combed and tightly rubber banded. I like them, their sweet alienness. If I mention Miss Carla while Martha's pushing the iron back and forth along the metal-colored cloth of the board, Martha will sigh and say nothing, and then get into the spirit of her version of gossip, a good-natured mixture of resignation and complaint.

I like her word for Miss Carla: a "tribulation." Miss Carla is a tribulation to her. Martha's assigned task is to respect her (as rich girl and employer's daughter) and control her at once, which both Martha and Carla know is impossible. Carla resists and ignores, and yet she must always be Miss Carla regardless. Therefore Miss Carla has won, particularly since she has long ago conquered the prime arena of her struggle for power, her mother. Her mother is Carla's chief accomplishment.

"Neighbor lady"—as opposed to referring to her by name—is

an economical means by which my parents convey disapproval almost entirely overshadowed by fascination. The elements of her character that are to be censured are precisely those that assure unflagging interest in her as a topic of conversation. She's a single mother, a term no one's thought of yet; the phrase of the hour is "out of wedlock," which has to be explained to me. "Neighbor lady" avoids the sticky problem of the appropriate prefix; would she be insulted by "Miss"? Does she defile the dignity of "Mrs."? To her face, they take the Southern tack of blurring her to a "Mizz."

She is or was, my mother says, the mistress of a Famous Jazz Musician from New Orleans. My mother inflects *New Orleans* in a way which makes that pretty name seem aligned with *Mistress*, a pair of soft words, against the hard and opaque opposite term, *wedlock*. As if they represented two cities, choices a person might make, the shadowy and slightly indecent New Orleans on the one hand, and plain well-lit wedlock on the other.

Mistress is evocative and inviting: sibilant, a little hissy. (I love the phrase *hissy fit* which is what people have when they get upset.) The word's tinged with a bit of Carla's mean streak, and her mother's lush burst of red hair, a color my mother maintains is nothing the Lord intended. She's often away; is she visiting the clarinetist? Is he the one who buys the outfits that rustle and shine in the dark of that closet, ensembles enough for an entire nine-year-old corps de ballet?

Probably it's the next day when I'm shown my father's stitches; probably I'd fallen asleep, next door, and someone's come to carry me home: sleepy body, up in the air over someone's shoulder; when you're carried, your face is that much closer to the sky. I know a little of what proceeds in great starry rotation over Memphis: Big Dipper, Little Dipper, Polaris, Milky Way. Or maybe it was that very night the wound was revealed to me, beneath its white shroud of gauze bandages, the suture displayed not as reminder of my guilt but as reassurance, so that I might understand the limit of what I've done, that it is specific and bounded: a jagged curve of black wire pulling together a violet seam along the pale underside of the foot, just the shape of the largest piece of glass.

Here my narrative vanishes in memory, gone underground like a stream. Or maybe now the scene shifts to some interior place: the classroom in the head, the room entirely lined with blackboards on which are chalked the characters I am learning to read, my version of an alphabet, gestures and figures translated to ideograms, star charts unreadable. Some adult says, *You couldn't help it*, but you're nearly asleep, aren't you; do you even hear? And now another interior space opens, not a schoolroom, though equally dark: a theater, on the strange promise of whose stage the Rainbow Girls are one by one making their appearance. In tulle and privacy, in tap shoes and spotlight, in a black glossier than all the night around her, in a wig wine-dark or flame or golden, each moves singly and shyly toward her debut.

2

A Book of Archaeology

For Christmas I receive a stocking taller than I am, made of red netting like the sort in which onions are bagged, only stronger, and stuffed with all manner of breakable and briefly interesting things, proving that the idea and experience of bounty is better than the specific components of abundance: little cars of fragrant plastic whose wheels turn on wire axles that can be popped loose and examined; hard candies; sweet, chalky wafers strung together into wristlets and necklaces. Small, provocative puzzles. These are shallow cylinders of cardboard, both ends sealed with a circle of hard plastic beneath which you can see a picture (a fat man with a beard, a circus seal atop a harlequin drum). In the pictures are little holes; in the cylinder are little steel balls, and the idea is to tilt and spin the sealed little world until the balls fall into place. The operation is delicate, and doomed, since a jostle means it's incomplete again, and anyway, if you "solve" one side, the other's in disarray.

We open our presents on Christmas Eve; my father and Sally take me for a walk, just after twilight, each holding one of my hands, and along the way my father says, "Hey, did you see that?" What? "That streak of red, that sleigh, didn't you see that flash? That was Santa Claus going by." My sister says she heard the jingle of sleigh bells. I don't believe in Santa Claus. But did I hear it? By the time we're home, the presents have come: elves' work, in bright dime-store papers, under the tree with its fat bulbs in the cheery simplicity of their crayon-box colors: blue and green, orange and red.

Too many lights outside, my mother says, make a house look honky-tonk. This year of the Daughters of the Eastern Star and having a maid who is at least partly ours, my mother seems to be interested in removing us from vulgarity. Or rather she's come to see other possibilities than she's known, and she has it in mind for us to align ourselves with that different life. And in fact the best of my presents is the most high toned, an oversize volume about archaeologists and their digs, each section devoted to a different culture, pages crowded with paintings of golden discoveries: horned and winged masks and vessels, and the earrings and breastplates of heroes and gods.

The book is so specific and resonant in my memory it still seems a physical presence; it fills my lap, the stiff boards of its bronzy cover emblazoned with a hodgepodge of Egyptian and Assyrian stuff, all covered with a thin glaze of something like cellophane which gradually begins to peel at the corners like sunburnt skin. *Open the heavy book*: a pointedly bookish smell (varnish? glue?), itself a little tomblike, redolent of stones and dust. Pages always cool as marble. The opening describes a dig, the work begun with pickaxes and spades and then continued, once the discoveries start, with spoons and hand brooms gradually whisking away earthen layers which cloaked the wonders the rest of the book was given over to: ancient things, compelling in their strangeness. Golden jackal's head, turquoise eye of the jaguar. A promise, a world or worlds beneath this one. And at the end of the long cool shafts, the empty passageways: the sealed chamber, the treasure.

❦

Childhood's work is to see what lies beneath. Under my family's surface, I could feel the buried foundations, the desires or disruptions, the longings and unfulfillments. I watched for the ways they'd push up, heave against the plain surface of the days. I learned to look out for the dangerous outcroppings, and if I couldn't know what they meant, I couldn't miss the ways these histories colored the present, intruding into today.

Aren't our parents always mysterious to us, mounded fields in which we can barely read the forming architecture beneath? What can't be seen troubles the earth, contours of an old city. *What* is buried? The child senses moments of pressure, outbreaks of something important. And later it's the same: even as adults, the work of understanding our parents is archaeological; what shaped them, we ask, who gave me shape? What's the history of the two people who are the origin of history, that shrouded beginning point whose evidence I handle now, holding the broken bits to daylight?

Begin with the stories they tell about themselves.

∾

I loved to draw, my mother says, *but there wasn't any paper. It was the Depression, in Sweetwater, in East Tennessee, and a drawing pad was a treasure. When I'd get one for Christmas I used to fill both sides of the pages. I drew squirrels and milk cans and barn cats and my father's wagon. My father was named Stephens, it used to be Van Stephens, because he was Dutch, and he had a full head of white hair till the day he died. My mother was Mary O'Cochran. Her mother came from Georgia to Tennessee in the back of a covered wagon when they heard that Sherman had reached the sea and turned and was coming back again; they'd survived the first march, and hidden the horses in a pit covered with brush, though the Yankee soldiers had stolen the bacon frying in the pan.*

I had so many brothers—roughhousing boys who'd fight in the barn—and then my sister Mildred, then me, the youngest. Though there was another sister too. My mother had two fine things: a tall blue vase she bought on her honeymoon at the St. Louis World's Fair in 1914, and a red velvet cape she called her "opera cloak." When my little sister died she cut up the cape and sewed her daughter a shroud. She doesn't say she had a baby who died herself, a blue baby born between Sally and me who would have been my brother; boy without a name, as

29
∾

F
i
r
e
b
i
r
d

far as I know, buried in some Tennessee cemetery in a grave nobody will ever visit.

❧

I was so skinny, my father says, *the boys used to get me into a corner of the school yard and feed me graham crackers to fatten me up. That winter we lived in a cabin in the woods we heated with an oil drum my Dad had found and cut a hole in to make a woodstove. We lived on squirrels we shot and cornmeal mush. To this day I hate cornmeal mush.* He doesn't say why they've come to Tennessee, he and his father, Orlin, and his mother, Lona. His father, an out-of-work carpenter, shot a man, a creditor who'd come to the door looking to collect, and killed him, or so Sally will tell me later. My father and his brother, Clarence (*always the perfect one, they always liked Clarence best*), learned to hit squirrels more often than not with the blue-black shotgun, and my father skinned them with his old pocketknife—rusty handle, oiled blade—peeling the fur back for whatever bits of stew meat a squirrel provides. We have this same shotgun for years—always?—leaning upright in a corner of my father's closet. He cleans and polishes it from time to time. I've taken it out myself, when I'm home alone, and held the oiled wood and heavy weight of it on my shoulder, looking down the long blue barrel.

❧

My father said he was taking the millet to be milled for flour, on his wagon, and had to drive through a darkish part of the woods. (This is my mother speaking.) *Then a man stepped out of the trees. My father slowed down to offer him a ride, but he didn't say a word, just swung himself up onto the wagon seat. My father tried to talk, but the man wouldn't speak. Nothing at all. Finally my father said, "Who are you?" and still the man said nothing. And then my father got scared, and said, "Get off of my wagon," but the man didn't move, and then your grandfather took the crop he used to drive the horses and went to strike the stranger—but the whip went right through him like he wasn't even there! He tried to hit him over and over again, but the phantom just got up and walked away into the trees. And we knew it was true, when my father came home, because the wagon seat was just slashed to ribbons, and who would ruin his own wagon?*

All my grandparents still lived on farms, and I'd been to visit my mother's people, where my Granny lived in a three-room wooden shack and kept a big stick by her bed in case she needed to club a snake in the night. My aunt Mildred made biscuits from dough rolled out, spread with butter fresh that morning from her churn, folded and rolled and folded again then cut into full moons which puffed, in the oven, to cream and golden astonishments, a dozen layers breaking apart in your hand like some heavenly shale.

We'd lived in the country too, with my father's parents—his mother reading the Bible on the front porch, calling me her sweetheart and wrapping me up in thin mottled arms, taking me with her out into the long slope of the fields to pick dandelion greens and poke salad, slipping me spoonfuls of Geritol to fatten me up. His father rocking, cutting plugs of tobacco and spitting the nasty juice into a can, wrapping his ankles in strange fleshy rubber stockings, and hoarding a drawer full of the most beautiful fountain pens, all swirled and marbled celluloid, though as far as I could tell he never wrote anything. Maybe an old account book, with the prices of feed and tobacco and ink recorded? We'd raised chickens there, and I used to watch my father use one hand to soothe a deluded hen, stroking it till it lay still on the stump, then raise the other to strike with one unswerving swing of his ax. Spurting blood smell, and then the hapless, beheaded thing running around crazily till it fell to one side in the dust, soon to be plucked and roasted. How can a body run without a head? Poorly, it would seem, in scrawly loops. Midday Sunday cooking: greens simmering with fatback, chicken roasting in a flecked black pan, mashed potatoes beaten with butter and milk, Crisco cut into flour for a latticed crust over a bubbly thick stew of red cherries. Hurry, please, the perfunctory grace.

But we'd lived in the new suburban places, too: Alcoa, where my father did something involving, of course, aluminum; Oak Ridge, where he was a night watchman at the nuclear plant; and Nashville, and towns that are nameless to me now. Towns where we could walk to shops, like the after-Christmas day my mother and I walked to Woolworth's, after Aunt Marguerite had sent me a card containing a dollar, and I discovered just how far a dollar might go: a wooden paddle with a pink rubber ball attached by stretchy elastic, a jigsaw puzzle of a windmill or waterfall (individual pieces cut to resemble Florida and the Liberty Bell), liquid stuff for bubble blowing, and this delightful object: a sheet of cardboard picturing a bald man under a plastic bubble, iron filings inside like so many shaved black hairs. When you moved a magnet attached by a piece of string, *voilà!*—spiky hair, beards, goatees. We walk home down Ramses Street, me carrying my big paper bag of things, the volume of them somehow more important than the particulars, past the stop signs and the parking lots, the lonely bench where black women waited for the bus.

∾

Your mother was raised a Catholic, my father says, *by her grandmother, who was from Ireland, but there wasn't any Catholic church; everybody was Presbyterian, and her brothers used to go to a little place called Fortner's Chapel. They kept snakes there, rattlesnakes to handle when they got to praying. Some of them got bit, but nobody died, not that I ever heard about. They didn't take to Catholics in Sweetwater, but the old lady took her off by herself and taught her the rosary and that kind of thing anyway. They'd pray to Mary, and everybody was hopping mad when they found out, but you don't tell an old Irish lady what to do. They must have been the only Catholics in East Tennessee. Your mother wanted to be Catholic later, but I wouldn't let her.*

∾

The world of the stories my parents told—the country world—was just imaginable to me, though already remote. Eating a squirrel, frying up a possum in a lean winter? It was a life they wanted to move away from, even as it comprised the chief substance of their language, their figures of speech, their songs.

We didn't sing popular songs like Giselle McKenzie sang on television: "Shrimp Boats" or "(How Much Is) That Doggie in the Window." (I like Giselle McKenzie, who seems beautiful and kind, even diminished in the small window of our TV screen in its big wooden box. I like her black hair puffed over her pale face, and her black dress à la Dior, the bell of the skirt a pedestal for her little waist, the simple black bodice. She tilts her head from side to side and smiles and sings at once, "Shrimp boats are a'comin', we're happy tonight. . . ." She suggests an approachable glamour: her pretty dress, shrimp cocktails in tall chilled glasses, the lucky members of "our studio audience." Someday I want to join a "studio audience." I like her much better than the dutifully cheerful Dinah Shore, who stretches her mouth to blow a big messy kiss at the screen, and tells us to "see the USA in a Chevrolet.")

We'd sit on the porch swing (said at each new address: *It isn't home till you hang the porch swing*), and in the loveliest hour, the gloaming, twilight deepening into evening, we sang hymns: "I Come to the Garden Alone," "Whispering Hope," "Rock of Ages." My mother always said, "I wish I could remember the one my mother used to sing, the one that goes, *He's a lily of the valley, he's a bright and shining star*," but she never did.

Now it seems extraordinary to me, our night singing, loud and completely unabashed. Imagine you are walking a quiet Memphis street, summer, nearly dark, the big shade trees alert with cicadas, fireflies dreamy over the lawns and ivies. Nothing distinguishes this house from the others but this homemade music. The father might join in, though more likely he's gone in to polish his shoes for tomorrow; the older sister's usually out somewhere—a date? But the mother and son are reliable, evening after evening. The woman just now forty and the boy recently six sing the doxology, though you wouldn't know that when it comes around to the line *Praise him all creatures here below*, the boy thinks of devils, underground things, that Creature from the Black Lagoon. *Swing low, sweet chariot, He is tramping out the vintage, Wait till the tempest is done.* They do every verse they know of "The Old Rugged Cross"; she teaches him all she can remember while they rock slowly and sing with abandon, so involved it never occurs to them what the neighbors might think, or to notice that you've stopped to watch, trying to guess their story. You wouldn't think that boy has a shred of self-consciousness, nor his mother, while they pour themselves into their duet: *I want to be in that number, when the stars refuse to shine.* By this time the fireflies are drowsing down near the roots of the hydrangeas, the darkness has cooled and solidified, and some late quality in the air signals that it's time to go in: *We'll sing again tomorrow.* Oh, stranger, did you ever hear such a pair?

My sister's new boyfriend, Jerry, has a motorcycle: a potent little package of chrome and black enamel that gives off some scent of heady thrill, intoxicating, like a stolen cigarette or the scent of bourbon. He's sleek as his machine, all of seventeen, muscular from working in his daddy's concrete business, his thick black hair oiled and combed back attentively, just the right lank flourish of curl in the front, loosely shadowing his forehead, pushed back sometimes with a veiny arm: *Love me tender*. Once Sally takes me to the pool with him; she's lying in the sun slick with Coppertone. (I am embarrassed by the Coppertone girl, the one whose white buttocks are exposed by the dog tugging at her bathing suit; where is her dignity?) Sally's going blonder, pointy white sunglasses like my mother's making her look unsettlingly adult, and I'm walking around the perimeter of the pool, when I come upon the damp windowless shed where the lifeguards and their buddies lift weights. Jerry's on his back on the bench, pressing a barbell up, his friends in their black trunks circled around him, just enough light through the cracked barnlike door so I can make out the oiled curves of the boys' chests and shoulders, their slim, dappled bellies in the dark hot room that seems to pulse with their combined presence, a room where I could never go, though I might stand struck still beside the door by something I couldn't name.

Another hot day, Jerry takes me for a ride on the back of the motorbike. His shirt's off, he's wearing just blue jeans, and in order to stay on the bike as we tool around corners, scooping the neighborhood, I am to put my arms around his bare waist, the likes of which I have never before touched: supple and chiseled, both firm and just yielding enough, sun colored, inexplicably satisfying, sending off some deep flutter in me, down in the base of my stomach, in the base of my spine—something far more exciting than riding a motorcycle.

This body is so different from my father's pale softness, from any other man I've seen (what other man have I seen?), the first male I've apprehended or touched who seems to me compelling, beautiful, his chest and belly themselves like some golden thing from Sumer, an artifact pulled from the burial mounds of Troy.

The origins of sexual feeling don't interest me much; they seem permanently shrouded anyway, as resistant to explanation as any form of desire: why, exactly, do you like strawberries? From whence springs your affection for the cello, your attraction to blue? I don't mean to be facetious; it's merely that by the time desire manifests itself it is *there*, a fact of the self, one of our well-springs. Genetics, hypothalamus, environment, chance, some inscription encoded in the DNA or the soul: your choice. Or no choice; doesn't the need to understand the origins of desire arise from the impetus to control it?

A far more productive field of inquiry is the way in which sexual feeling makes itself known, and how we negotiate with our sense of desire, and with the dawning awareness of difference.

Here's a story told to me by Warren, a participant in a writing workshop I taught in Astoria, Queens, in a church basement called the SAGE Clubhouse—"SAGE" stands for Senior Action in a Gay Environment—where gay and lesbian senior citizens gather for meals and classes. We sat in a circle of folding chairs in a corner, drinking coffee from Styrofoam cups and eating the cookies Rudy and Frank had baked while everyone told wonderful stories: Harlem rent parties in the forties, meeting a first boyfriend in the trenches during the Second World War, and long, tender couplings of decades.

Sixty years before, as a second- or third-grader, Warren sat beside a boy whom he admired, a popular and handsome kid, and one day Warren noticed something he had never before observed. When the handsome boy wore a polo shirt, his arm filled the sleeve, so that the fabric stretched a little. Warren's arms did not fill a sleeve in this way; it had never occurred to him that an arm *could* fill a sleeve, and in observing this characteristic of the boy's body Warren realized that he found it remarkable; the muscle, in its taut encasement of cloth, was a beautiful thing.

Struck by what he had seen, Warren told another boy, a friend, and was startled by his friend's indifference to this matter: no response. After school, puzzled, he also told his mother about the beautiful arm, and she responded with a discussion of the variations in human body types, how some are naturally more muscled than others. Her intention was to reassure Warren that his body was acceptable, which was not what he was after. He knew what he felt, in the thrall of the swell of that boy's bicep. He understood, through some echo beneath her speech, unstated but perfectly clear, that he'd apprehended beauty in a location she did not approve.

Message: there are private forms of loveliness, there are things about you no one should know. Should you be ashamed, to see what others cannot? Does the delight—your new, secret possession—outweigh your sense of singularity?

Or does the shame simply commingle with the pleasure, infusing it with something airless, covetous, irremediably solitary: the boy alone in the hothouse of his loves?

∾

Sally comes home with a new haircut. Wisely she's told no one of her plan; her longish blond hair is gone, the sides now combed back like a boy's: *Love me tender*. The haircut, all the rage, is called the DA, a polite acronym for duck's ass, since the hair in the very back curls up in a saucy point. (Sometime around 1975 hair ceased to have the social and political meanings it once carried in America; dreadlocks or shaved heads or blow-dried stylings still announce our social allegiances, but the signifying potency of Sally's gesture is hard to feature now, when it would be just one more gesture toward fashion. In 1959 a DA was about class, femininity, and rebellion in a big way, so Sally has broken a rule—another one I didn't know existed—and all hell's broken loose.)

Mother's in the kitchen, smoking and weeping; she hates the phrase "DA" and actually seems to prefer "duck's ass," though she lowers her voice on the second word and utters it with a bit of a hissing shudder. Her eyes are a tired red. My father's entire face is red. He yells, smolders, sputters, and smolders more, but the deed is done. Sally sulks in her room, too wounded even to play records or write in her white five-year diary with the little golden key. She is triumphant but miserable. Old photos of my sister are brought out, childhood pictures in which, in pinafore and long straight hair, she resembles the Alice of the Tenniel illustrations for *Alice in Wonderland*; her whole name is in fact Sarah Alice. No more; this haircut says *hood*, says *greaser*, spells *trouble*. Motorbikes, biceps, and DAs say, *Good-bye Wonderland, good-bye Rainbow Girls, hello rock 'n' roll.*

Tattoos and a life of dissipation cannot be far behind. The unspoken issue (unspoken in front of me, anyway) is sex: Sally's done what she likes with her body, and the implications are clear, and somehow her freedom seems my parents' undoing. (We'll replay this scene, in 1969, over my own *lack* of a haircut, my own announcement that my body is mine.)

They have, in fact, been awful to her: even I can see this, and perhaps that's one reason I'm such a good boy, observant, spying out the unstated rules: I want to please them, but I'm afraid of them, too. One night she'd come home late, with a boyfriend before Jerry, and did I dream that commotion in the night? Shouting, the squirrel-killing gun pulled from the closet—now *there's* a boy who'll never show up around here again. And once some boy had given her a young boxer, a sweet, feisty scrapper of a dog I adored—Sally's pet, of course, but I'm not yet in school, home all day, and he's mine when she's gone. He's all chest, bandaged ears upright, shiny muscled flanks, and I name him Buster, after the boy pictured in ads for Buster Brown shoes; I have a pair of such shoes myself, and when we bought them I was given the gift of a plastic egg, which opened to reveal something completely forgettable. On one of our singing evenings, the dog had jumped up onto the swing where my mother and I sat, wanting to sit in a lap; he caught a paw between the painted green slats, panicked when my mother tried to extricate him, and bit a bruised half-moon onto the skin of her upper arm. The next day we were packed into our green Studebaker, the slender metal bar in the windshield up front dividing the world into yes and no, father and mother, dog and no dog. Sally and I sat in the back with the boxer between us, and my father drove out into the country someplace, a long way from home. He pulled over, got out, and took the dog from Sally's arms and set it down in the grass by the side of the asphalt—tall grass, dandelions, and wild white carrots. Then he got back in the driver's seat, slammed the door behind him, and drove away. Did we look back, Sally and I? Maybe the dog was already off into the brush, exploring, so that if we looked we wouldn't even see him get smaller as the car hurried away.

Why are my parents so mean to my sister? I am a good boy, a model child, which doesn't mean the kind of model I wanted to be in the silvery glass of Sally's bureau mirror. They tell Sally they wish she could be like me, which of course has the effect of alienating us from each other; how can I be her confidant if I am the adored example? I've been made complicitous with them. They've decided long ago she's a wild girl, in need of control, and if they aren't strict she's headed to the bad. But their strictness seems crazily contradictory: act like a nice girl or there'll be a shotgun at the door to welcome you home. What are they punishing her for? Desire? Autonomy? Something about her newness, how she's right at home in a world where they themselves seem to lack friends or know the rules? Sally's new hair means she fits, cool, part of a group, and they don't like that about her. They would like her to act like a young lady and thus avoid some imagined fate, something they've feared or are trying to leave behind? Maybe they're afraid she'll wind up being a white-trash girl in a laundromat, a bunch of babies stowed in some trailer park out on the edges of town, where there aren't any Daughters of the Eastern Star.

We lived, just one summer, in a big old rented house in the middle of a trailer park. I was friends with two identical little blond twins, boys named Clarence and Darence; they used to play in diapers or training pants, yellow from the tops of their heads to their urine-stained pants to their suntanned feet. Their trailer smelled like pee and laundry soap; they were boring but the fact of their being double offered some mildly sustaining interest. My parents couldn't wait to get out of the trailer park. The day we moved I was playing with Clarence and Darence in our yard, a plot of lawn not yet swallowed by mobile homes. Being a good host, I invited Clarence and Darence to come along with us in the Studebaker to see our new house, an action which provoked from my father a display of rage that made no sense to me at all, a scene which culminated in that single, unforgettable spanking, on a screened-in porch, painted a medicinal pale green, his face as red as if someone had a hand around his throat and were choking him, while he held me wriggling up in the air and said, "Don't you ever . . . "

Don't ever what? Make friends with the kids in the trailer park? Become the kind of person who could have friends in mobile homes?

Maybe my parents are afraid they won't be who they want to be, if their daughter's a bad girl. Probably a DA means she will soon be fallen, has fallen already? Are they just afraid that they will lose her? *I fell for Jerry, and Jerry really fell for me.* I don't like falling, but sometimes I court it anyway: Carla and I play a game in the yard where we spin and spin, arms spread out wide like dervishes, until we plop on the grass and feel the world go on whirling around us. Is that how it is for Sally, a dizzy new way of making things spin?

∽

My father says he fell in love with my mother on a picnic, in a park in Sweetwater next to the cemetery, when a dog came running out of the graveyard with a bone in its mouth. *Other girls would have found it macabre*, he says, *but your mother just laughed and laughed.* It's almost impossible for me to imagine my parents so young, not yet irrevocably joined to each other. These are the days of the New Deal, the slow upswing out of the Depression, and my father and his brother are working for the Civilian Conservation Corps, building stone stairways and picnic shelters in state parks, lining hiking trails with logs: make-work projects to put bread on the table and stop the economic hemorrhaging. Uncle Clarence—the bolder one, more socially at ease—dates my mother first, and that's how my father meets her. At first she thinks he's awkward and a little funny, but then he keeps hitchhiking to Sweetwater from the CCC camp to take her out, persistent, sort of goofily fun, evidently capable of devotion. She's been sick, some sort of influenza or rheumatic fever, which has kept her down nearly a whole year; she's thin, and though she's recovering she's kept a slight pallor warmed by the flush on her cheeks: a slightly fevered look, mildly tubercular, which my father finds irresistible.

Here he is, in a photo on my desk, a sharp-focused black-and-white studio portrait in a frame of gray cardboard, which unfolds to display and support the picture, rimmed by a narrow silver bevel. He's appealingly good-looking, not movie star looks but a sensuousness and a quality of alert presence which don't strike me as having much to do with the man as I've known him. It's the clarity of the large eyes, which look off to the right as though toward the future. The full lips lean startlingly toward the voluptuous: a bit of sexual smolder? And he has hair! Already thinning but still darkly respectable, combed with just the right degree of carelessness: he's got other things on his mind. I cover parts of his face to see if anything of my own visage is recognizable; not the eyes, or the rather aquiline nose, certainly not those lips. There: I have his ears. I search the photo and frame: no date, no penciled inscription. Just *Harding Studio, Cookeville* in a florid, Victorian-looking script. He is made younger, in his hopeful suit, by the affecting combination of optimism and vulnerability he projects; he's a young man, and who knows what the future might bring?

In the next photograph that future has arrived; his smile and tilt of the head say that whatever it was that was coming is here, and good. His hairline's receded a little, though at the crest of his forehead there's still enough to comb up into a jaunty, asymmetrical peak. The photo is tinted, so his suit jacket's an unlikely teal, his tie a watery blue and bronze; his blue eyes, narrowed a little, address the camera head-on, the lips seeming less wide now that they're parted in a smile. As in some old Dutch painting, some antique wedding portrait, his head and shoulders form one shape with the woman beside him, her shoulder placed just before his, the two of them defining a jigsaw-edged field of white space behind them.

Of course what the boy in the first picture was awaiting was my mother, and certainly she shines, in this souvenir picture (*Cline Studios,* scrolled on the paper frame with its artful little deckle of paper fringe, *Chattanooga, Tenn.*) with a radiant intensity which makes her seem larger than her body, as if she's the picture's actual source of light.

Her hair's brushed back from her rather high forehead into soft waves, more curls at the back of her neck, artfully bunched, not touching her shoulders; has she seen Garbo in *Camille*? No, *Gone With the Wind.* She and her mother read the book twice, and cried both times. Then they waited in a line that stretched around a city block in Knoxville to see the movie, and cried again. My mother must have *felt* that dirt in Scarlett O'Hara's fist when she shook it at the Technicolor sunset and swore she'd never be hungry again. And the identification wasn't only personal; book and film elegized a world lost when Atlanta burned, a dream, and my mother and my granny loved it. Though their family was never invited to crinolined gatherings at Tara or Twelve Oaks; immigrants, sharecroppers, they cherished the myth anyway, a Southern golden age. "People don't understand," my mother said, "that the Southerners were *good* to their slaves."

In the photo she's wearing a jacket with slightly padded shoulders, a complicated coral paisley accented with auburn and blue, a matching blouse beneath it. Her face is what the fashion magazines describe as egg-shaped, its ovoid punctuated by her blue gaze. how careful here, the tinter's brush, limning the iris, the tiny corners of the whites of her eyes. The face is anchored and sparked by her smile: beautiful, unchecked, no hesitation in it, framed by her thin, perfectly painted lips, the upper lip especially narrow, like mine. Here is the source of the particular intensity with which she commands the frame: her smile and her eyes don't quite align, the dazzle of one just so subtly opposing the depth of the other: delight and—what? Something withheld, not yet available to us? Something, unlike that smile, which is unwilling, unready to be known.

They are so like my sister's eyes!

Strange how the picture changes if you look only at their eyes: suddenly he seems a little wary, she a little wily, a bit more knowing than that bright, uncompromised smile would lead one to think. Perhaps it's only the tilt of his head, or the arch shapes of her plucked eyebrows, or maybe it's nothing at all. Taken at face value, their whole bright faces, they are astonishingly and forthrightly happy, lit up by pleasure in a way in which I will never see them, not quite, and a little wave of shock attends the recognition that she is all of seventeen, and he merely twenty-three; I feel protective toward them, want to keep them right here, in this bright moment in Chattanooga sixty years ago, the flash of the photographer's lamp finding its match in their unmistakable joy.

∽

The ducktail incident seems mild next to what follows, that loudly articulated disapproval far preferable to what settles over our house: strain, silence, a heaviness infecting everything, the steam iron moving back and forth over the board deliberately, so slow as to seem calculated, even murderous. The air's fogged with Salems, and my memory seems cloudy, too, perhaps because of our household's palpable sense of tension and of gloom, or perhaps because now things happen in such a hurry. The word *pregnant* is never spoken; a wedding is announced; somewhere in the rush of things my mother says to me, "Your sister has to get married," a statement fraught with depths I can't sound.

Sally takes me to the movies, to see *The Ten Commandments*, a big event; a huge red curtain pulls back to reveal a prologue, in which Cecil B. DeMille tells us how important this all is, and then there's Egypt, in Technicolor, baby Moses in the bulrushes. I like this; I know this story from Sunday school. I like the way the child floats to safety, and the secrecy of his identity; no one knows he's a prophet, a miracle maker. I enjoy the plagues: snakes and blood and lightning and bare-chested Yul Brynner as Pharaoh carrying the body of his son, and I like the Red Sea parting like the red curtain, but the movie goes on and on, Israelites in the wilderness, and I have to pee and somehow feel I shouldn't say so. Outside, waiting for my father to come pick us up, I wet my pants and Sally's annoyed with me, but then she tells me about her wedding dress anyway, not a dress actually but a suit: very modern, as she presents it, and simple, in beige brocade, with a beige pillbox hat sporting its own small beige veil.

Beige? Couldn't somebody give the girl a nice white dress? If my parents chose it, it seems a way of marking her shame, of observing some code of honor bizarrely more important than their daughter. If *she* chose it, it seems like Hester Prynne's gesture: wear your shame, girl, put it in their faces, and look beautiful while you go about it; you stand up there and you look perfect.

And she does. And him, midcentury Apollo in a tux, dimpled, devastating smile. The wedding's a blur: my little family but lots and lots of Jerry's people—"the Lowells" as my parents call them, as though they were an undifferentiated mass. The Lowells seem unreservedly happy about the whole thing, although my parents contend the Lowells believe Jerry to be marrying beneath him. They say the Lowells think we're not high-class enough for them; because those Lowells own a cement business, they have their noses in the air. Is anyone taking pictures? Is this occasion something for my parents other than—Martha's word again—*tribulation*? Cake in the church basement. Strain. Strain and duty.

But of course there's a wedding picture, and it's here my sister's eyes exactly mirror my mother's, in that long-ago wedding portrait: these eyes say, these girls knew what they were doing, these girls married to get out. Did either of them know what their eyes revealed, or did they experience their courtships as love untempered by any other motive? Maybe my sister's trapped in something she doesn't want, certainly in something she isn't old enough to manage, but she's found a way to take the next step. *Pregnant* means nobody's going to stand in her way.

And it's no time before my parents announce that we're moving—this time someplace entirely new. My father has been transferred and we are going to Arizona. To the desert, like the Israelites. And we do go, but not before Sally has her baby, a beautiful girl named Lisa, born with dark, luxuriant hair. I'm fascinated and repelled by the umbilicus, dark little shriveling casing on her belly. She seems at once the newest and oldest thing in the world, and in that way has some odd connection to my favorite book, in which antique things seem perennially new and strange, even though looking at them also makes them more ancient. The movers tag each box with a number before it goes into the big Mayflower truck. Sally lives in an apartment now, with Jerry and Lisa, but I don't think I've ever been there. I'll bring my book along in the car, in which I cannot take much. It is good for long trips, since the pictures lend themselves so readily to dream. My favorites are, just now, these great Assyrian horse-men, immense and imperturbable: their huge and noble flanks, their confident, unreadable smiles.

3

Beast from the Year 5000

Maybe the movie wasn't like this at all, maybe I've completely invented it. But this is how I remember it: the Lyric Theater, on the edge of the barrio in downtown Tucson, and I'm somewhere between second and third grade, somewhere between seven and eight. In those days, 1960 or so, the Lyric isn't the derelict place it'll soon become, the last of the moviehouses still unrazed. A decade later, I'll get beaten up here, in this same cool darkness, in the front row, kicked in the head by a gang of black kids who smash my glasses and knock my friend's tooth out, but that's another world from *this* Lyric. Though it's already down-at-the-heels enough to be showing a movie like this on a Saturday afternoon, is it? Must be, since my father can take me during the daytime. What does he do while I'm studying monsters? *I'm going to read my book*, he says, *I'm going to run some errands*, or, *I'll just nap in the shade.* I am to go to the glass-and-chrome box of the ticket booth and ask what time the movie is over. The cashier answers through the round hole beside her mouth; I run back and tell my father, then he's gone, and I buy my ticket and make my way into the cool lobby, to the candy counter, and then through the theater's padded double doors.

I like this privacy, like to be alone in the silvered and variable dark, the velvet curtain billowing down from the elaborate plaster arch of the proscenium, even the little patch on the screen, white on white, where someone's thrown something up there that broke the stretched emulsion of illusion. I like having a full box of something in my lap—Jujubes (the fruit flavors on the edge of bitter, and they stick to your teeth annoyingly, but they last a long time). Hard dollops of Milk Duds, only glancingly chocolate. It doesn't matter; what one wants is the satisfaction of something to suck until absorption in the film takes over. Sometimes, even often, this never takes place, since I will see any movie, even boring ones: dull John Wayne in *Donovan's Reef*, wide-eyed Debbie Reynolds as *Tammy* singing that awful syrupy song in a swamp, even *Snow White and the Three Stooges*, which I confess I enjoy a little—some skating star smiling in her short fur-trimmed skirt and spinning on a studio pond in drifts of cottony snow—despite the three tiresome clowns.

I prefer films about monsters. Once, in a glass case in the tiled wedge of vestibule beside the ticket booth, this poster: a leanly muscled man kneels, bare chested, while a woman in a tight blouse writhes, in thrall to a warty, greenish heap like a cross between a cucumber and a haystack. Scary red letters, the print almost throbbing: Every Woman Its Mistress, Every Man Its Slave. In the movies I love, the body's mutable, untrustworthy. The werewolf's clothes are ripped apart by the pressure of his own exploding flesh. A teenage boy, shirtless, a potent physical presence, his face obscured by bandages, and when the wrappings on his head are removed he's become terrible, a Frankenstein. The amazing colossal man is so huge he has no choice but to be nearly naked as he stalks toward Hoover Dam; where did he find that immense loincloth which conceals his shame?

What is it I love in these awkward pageants of transformation and terror?

I am here to satisfy what the Buddhists call my "painted

hunger." The phrase comes from an old parable. An ancient Buddha said, "A painted rice cake does not satisfy hunger." But Dōgen, a commentator on this bit of wisdom, inverts it and makes it wiser, asserting that nothing in the world is any *more* real than that painted rice cake. "The entire phenomenal universe and the empty sky," he writes, "are nothing but a painting." For him all of reality is equally illusory, a flimsy pageant of desire and attachment.

"Since this is so," he continues, "there is no remedy for satisfying hunger *other* than a painted rice cake. Without painted hunger you never become a true person."

Wouldn't Dōgen have loved the movies then, with their false and flickering realms! That's what I am doing, becoming a person in the dark, in the worn red plush of my seat, lost in the projected hungers on the screen, the misshapen forms. The houselights dim; a uniformed usher with a flashlight comes to shush the kids down the aisle; the music ends, the Lyric's black vault suddenly pierced by a constantly mutating beam of light, brighter and lesser threads braiding together as this film flares and gathers itself, titles in tall white letters rushing up out of a black field: *Beast From the Year 5000.*

Here's the story. Some scientists who work at a laboratory in a little canyon have made a box of steel and glass, with a big adjustable dial on the front; it might be a version of the sleek ticket booth outside the Lyric, near the sidewalk. But this is a time machine; they set the dial for the past, turn it on, and the moon-shaped window of the chamber fills with fog. When the dry-ice vapors clear, lo! there's something in the box, a very old stone tool, chipped around the edges, something retrieved from Neanderthal days. The scientists are astonished, or as much so as these earnest actors can seem, in turbid black and white, in heavy dialogue.

Now they set the dial for the future, the fog blooms again, then thins to reveal: what? An elongated form, biomorphic, black, rather Danish Modern: it is a vase, of some as-yet-unknown material. The machine has reached far into the future and snatched a vase!

That's enough excitement for one day. The scientists yawn and go home, switching off the lights in the lab behind them. The sun goes down over the canyon; leaves are tossed by a wind, their undersides rippling silver; a coyote lifts his ears, watchful. Back in the lab an unsettling music begins, and we see that the dial of the time machine is still set at the year 5000 A.D. Our window into tomorrow fills with fog as before—but what is that gloved and sequined hand reaching from the vapors?

The Beast, of course, and the Beast is a woman. Or female, anyway, in a sparkling and hooded black bodystocking, all dimly gleaming waist and breasts, angling along in a sort of slo-mo sideways locomotion, elbows held way out from her body, long-nailed fingers spread wide, head to one side like a model's, slowly turning, all arrogance and futurity. Now her music's an oscillation between a wail and a high-pitched electronic drone: *Wooo-wooo, veee-veee.* She moves through the lab and out into the moonlit evening; her head's still turned just to one side, but her eyes scroll back and forth to take in what is to her the ancient world. The black upper reaches of the trees shudder now; coyote howls and the crickets cease. We've forgotten there's a security guard outside, at the wire fence's barbed gate; he rises from his little booth. Has he heard that unnerving music? He says, "What the. . . ." Close-up of his face filling with terror, fear commingled with pleading: have mercy. But she is mercilessness itself; she kills with a touch to the neck, black glove alive with little flashes of light as two fingers find his throat, as if she killed with sparkle.

Now, goodbye, coyote.

Reader, picture this high-ceilinged chapel, circa 1962, lit by beast light, and also, softly, by the red glow of exit signs at aisle's end, a few dim lamps beneath the metal armrests of the chairs on either side of the aisle, the whole space filled with the repetitive and thrumming music of fear. This box of a theater might itself be a foggy time machine, or Samuel Von Hoogstraten's perspective box, a distortion of light, and surely it must be a distortion, this nearly empty space with its echo of old grandeur, the strange film which makes little sense, and the boy who is too young to be here alone with his box of candy, his jacket on the seat beside him.

In this perspective box, two lenses are provided for us, two ways to view this chamber of instruction.

The first is in the back of the room, looking out over the boy's head to the screen itself, and it allows us to see the film with a new clarity, not for its surface, which is schlock, something turned out for boys to watch on Saturday or Sunday afternoons, for lonely drive-ins in the country, places to offer little attention to the unfolding mysteries on the screen, the decade's funny nightmares playing themselves out up there in monochrome or heated Technicolor.

But say this lens allows us to see beneath the surface, to what compels the child's attention, and how shall I tell you that? There is the matter of archaeology, something pulled up from the past. There is the matter of the box's generative quality, how it produces from fog both evidence of the lost world and a sleek, unreadable thing from the future: images of art's power, how something never before seen appears, in the heightened realm of the box. The oldest thing in the world, the newest thing.

But of course there's more than that: the hooded woman, who walks sideways through the world, who glistens darkly, who is— evil? Charged, certainly, with some negative prospect, a terrifying force. When she touches people they die, and I the boy viewer am disappointed by that. Not much of a monster, if all she does is touch. But through the lens we see that makes her *more* of a monster, and tragic—that what she touches is poisoned, tarnished somehow, compromised. Of course she's the boy's mother, or a painted rice-cake version of her, and of course he finds her both fascinating (those chill sequins, the glamour of her hood) and scary; why must she walk like that in the world, what is that edgy music which accompanies her?

Of course I'm in love with my mother, as befits a sensitive young man. A tired old whiff of Freudian fog hangs about the love of a gay son for his mother, but let us here attempt to dispel it: loving her so ardently is a result, not a cause. The old dominant mother theory puts the cart before the pony: I am not a gay boy because I am obsessed with my mother; it's that my mother looms monumental *because* I'm drawn to her potent mix of emotional vulnerability and made surfaces. She is the dominant emotional figure in the landscape; she seems so much more profound and complicated than any man I've known. And she has legitimate access to the stuff of craft, the tools with which beauty is made.

And there's more; the lens always can take us a little further. I love my mother more because it isn't safe to love her. You can't trust her mercurial unavailability, unpredictable alternations of affection and absence. Taut, contained surface, withdrawal. Then a wash of affection: *you're the center of the world, what could you ever do wrong?* There's a particular hold love has over you when you're afraid of who you love.

∾

One day I'm playing in the desert with my friend Kurt. Our games have to do with digging in the dry arroyos—sometimes we find shards of old pottery there, terra-cotta-colored fragments, inscribed with wavy lines—digging under the hot sand to the cool sand, and saying dirty words. Kurt teaches me a new vocabulary; we look at the smutty pictures other kids have drawn on the concrete walls beneath a bridge that crosses the dry wash. I ask what *Fuck* means and Kirk explains, incorrectly. We pee in a little metal tea strainer we've found; we say, *Shit*. It feels interestingly powerful to say it. We walk to my house and, coming into the shade of the carport—I don't know my mother is at the kitchen window, just a few feet away—I say, "Shit."

All hell breaks loose. She is disappointed in me, thought I was a nice boy, a smart boy; she is furious. She spanks the backs of my thighs with the hard back of a hairbrush, she considers making me eat soap. We are alone together in the house, and the kitchen and the dining area are full of her anger, steely and overbearing, and still feeling that taste of power I've gotten from strong words, I say, "I hate you."

Now hell collapses into something worse. She's at the sink, pretending to wash the dishes, she is rigid with recrimination, somewhere between tears and fury. She wants me out of her sight; she says, "I didn't know that's how you feel, I've done nothing but love you, I've been nothing but good to you, but if that's how you feel . . . "

Now I've done the worst thing, there's nothing more terrible than this, I have wounded the woman I love; she will never forgive me, she has turned the sun of her affections away from me forever. I get down on my knees in the kitchen, in the center of the room ringed by the new avocado cabinets, I am reaching out toward her waist, I say, "Please, forgive me, I didn't mean it, you must forgive me."

And she rolls her eyes at my performance. Something about this is terrible: she is embarrassed by the pitch of my emotions, so suddenly we're both self-conscious, aware that we're playing a scene. I am too dramatic, the depths of my feelings are disserved by my falsity, as if she can see right then clearly, unmistakably, that I'm a little drama queen, that I'm not going to turn out to be who she thought. But I'm not false, am I? How else plead my Proustian love, which is intensified by rejection? Am I too much like her? She hisses, "Get off your knees."

∾

There's no father in the movie. Perhaps the father is all these men who have conjured the beast from the distant future, all these ineffectual technicians and scientists. What have they brought into the world, deadly, out of control, silent, stalking at twilight for her own mysterious purposes? What does she want with the past, anyway, what does she want with these men? Nothing, really, they are annoyances, merely in the way of her inscrutable purpose.

∾

And there's something else, too; always more to the story. It's not just that the beast is a figure for his mother, with her strange alloy of the glamorous and the malefic, like Maleficent, the horned mother in Disney's *Sleeping Beauty*, also in black, her gestures also dangerous and entrancing. The Prince fights his way through a wall of thorns, his white flesh pricked and made paler by a few drops of blood, but the ram-horned Mother only laughs and raises her lightning-forked staff to summon her dragon.

She isn't just a symbol for the boy. He wants to *be* her, too, a werewoman from the other side. He wants to walk through the world wearing her otherness, wants those sequins and those strange curves, the sleekness of something *designed*, like a car or a Danish vase, something steely, something streamlined that perhaps doesn't immediately reveal its purpose, something modern. She's power and artifice and allure, an object of fascination— which means, really, that she's in him already. He contains what he wants to become: an alien woman from the future, chilly queen from space who will move obliquely through this world, killing the men who try to encumber her.

∾

And through the other lens, the one I've positioned on the screen of the Lyric Theater, from which the movie looks out at the boy? What does the lens reveal about him?

Sitting close to the screen—he needs glasses, and will have them before too long, but no one's yet figured out that he can't see well, and he himself does not understand that the world looks different to anyone else—he is too young. People don't think so much about danger to children, not in '61 or '62, but he is still a little boy; where is his father, who's dropped him at the curb two hours ago, or is it a double feature this time? Is it so they can be away from *her*, away from home, in this beat downtown already emptied out? The sprawl of suburbs turn their back on the failing center of the city, the only place here where things are *old*.

What I can tell you, what I can see most clearly about this child, is that he is absolutely, plainly alone, clutching the candy he hopes will last the entire duration of the film. He's lived in seven houses in seven years. He's a little pudgy, eager to pour his attention out of his body up onto the screen. His grandparents are dead or far away; his big sister's a teenage girl with two kids now, in another state, so it's him and his parents, who don't seem to have any friends, who keep moving, disconnecting, and whom he already knows he can't tell about a world of things inside him. Maybe it isn't just them; maybe that's what it is to be a person, all these dreams and apprehensions and questions you can't say to anybody. Either because you lack a vocabulary for them, or because no one would understand if you did say them, since the interior of each person seems to be a separate place, as if everyone were permanently alone at the movies, watching their own silvery interiority up on some private screen while the dazzling afternoon goes on outside.

So he's gotten good at being alone, since that is where he is and where he is going to be, and it isn't the worst thing, is it? The movie-house daydream, a new book—he hopes they will carry him entirely, the story possessing him, its large life overwhelming his smaller one: it will tell him what to see, for exactly ninety minutes, the stream of things ordered into a story—he loves that. Anxiety, watching previews: is that what I'll have to watch, is that all I will be offered? I need to see something, is this all there is to see? A kind of desperation in it: please bring me something scary, something absorbing, because I don't have a choice but to see the movie . . . .

In the movies you're by yourself (even when you're with someone, you're by yourself) but not lonely. Is that a boon or a sadness? He's sealed, away from the parents, in a glass coffin like Snow White's, some chamber they can't penetrate: fog-filled time machine, impervious cage of the ticket booth. Mother and father can't touch him here.

Or did they put him in the chamber? Get him out of the way for a while, get him out of the way for good: send him off to the world of art, send him into shadowland. But he likes it there, resilient boy, though right now the lens seems to make him smaller and smaller, the only figure in all those rows. The screen is huge—movie houses weren't divided then, just empty places bigger than any space I knew—so my weekend afternoon monsters were immense, daunting. What did it matter what they did or said? They were twenty feet tall. I, immense now, more present than that boy, an eye turned to scrutinize the way he's wrapped his jacket around him to warm up, the jacket he'll of course lose at the movies, I look at him and find him a distortion of a child my lens cannot correct.

4

Mikey

We live on East Twenty-second Street, a busy thoroughfare, on a strip of low-slung cinder-block ranch houses where there aren't many trees to absorb the heat. Some of our neighbors have given up on lawns like the ones they had back East and gone to tinted gravel instead, and in the median strip that divides the whizzing traffic on East Twenty-second the town crew's actually painted the dry grass a pale, chemical green. Some afternoons sandstorms blow up, "dust devils" my parents call them, but these cyclones aren't made of dust but of gritty sand, stinging, blinding; they don't last long but we kids caught out in them must double over, cover our faces, run to any shelter, but even then our faces and bare legs feel scoured.

I've made two friends.

Linda is tiny, blond, amazingly thin; we like each other immediately, though I am not sure just what brings us together. Partly it's that I like her name; back in Tennessee, when we'd rented a farmhouse in the middle of acres of field roamed by our landlord's horses, I'd named one spotted Appaloosa pony Linda, busy imagining relationships with horses that weren't mine and that I wasn't supposed to touch. One of them used its big yellow teeth to scrape the paint off the fenders of our Chevrolet.

Linda is a little frail looking, not so quick to speak up, and probably she's a good match for a new boy, a stranger with a thick Tennessee accent newly added to the roster of the second grade months after the beginning of the school year. If she were to draw her self-portrait she'd be a wisp of a thing, tucked into some corner of the page; somehow this makes her seem open, available; she seems to look at the world as though it will impose itself upon her in whatever way it chooses. One day Linda comes to my house to play, and my mother serves us lunch: Swanson's chicken pot pies, lovely bland childhood comfort food, mostly gravy and peas, a few chunks of chicken aswim in translucent thickened sauce and pieces of crust. Linda is amazed, her eyes huge; at her house, she says, one of these pies is cut into slices and divided for everyone in the family. When I go to her house, it's true; we have a tiny lunch, a fraction of a bologna sandwich. I imagine her at the dinner table, tiny girl with a wedge of pot pie on her plate, just a small radius of crust with its mechanically crimped edge.

I like playing with Linda: easy, no pressure. She seems to regard anything pleasant that comes her way as a surprise, not a given. We are considerate of each other; we invent quiet games; we are cooperative. One of my teachers says to my parents, on open house night, when a particularly silly-looking drawing of a reindeer I've done is tacked to the bulletin board, all sausage body and spindly legs and huge antlers, *Mark relates so well to girls.*

And I do, or at least better than I do with most boys, who seem already possessed of forms of knowledge opaque to me, things they grasp and I do not: baseball gloves, for instance, the inflation of rubber balls, marbles, the choosing of teams, names of models of cars. Where they got this knowledge I don't know; already I have a dawning sense that either it is too late for me to ask the questions or that questioning is not the way such understandings are gained. If you have to ask the rules of the boys' world, you can't possibly be one of the people who has the answers. To ask would betray my hopeless ignorance.

Or maybe I don't want to know.

During one of my parents' sporadic attempts to make friends, we go to visit a man with whom my father works, another Army engineer also engaged in the huge project of building under-ground silos in the desert, gigantic holes lined with corrugated metal, which will house white rockets tipped with nuclear war-heads. The engineer—handsome, in blue jeans and tight white T-shirt, warm in an unselfconscious way I am not used to—lives with his wife and son in a white trailer I think fascinating: such a long and narrow house, full of hiding places to stow things away. My fa-ther and his friend talk and drink some beers, my mother and the friend's wife tour the trailer and talk in the kitchen, and then all of them sit outside in folding green-webbed lawn chairs and talk, while I am to play with the son. He is my age and All Boy, smitten to the core with astronauts, the current pursuit and obsession of All Boys.

Thus, toy rocket ships, to scale, with realistic details, each of which must be pointed out; toy figures of Gus Grissom and Wally Schirra, star charts and posters depicting orbital patterns, the boy's trailer bedroom stuffed to bursting with the ephemera of space ex-ploration. Narrations of interesting facts, anecdotes, startling fig-ures (do you know how much you weigh in space? Nothing!). Worst of all, ludicrous to my mind, is the helmet, not just a plastic costume version but an incredibly elaborate affair, a wearable white bubble with clear acrylic visor and spiral patterns of little holes beside the ears. I want nothing to do with the helmet, but the boy wants only to put it on and roar around, immersed in his private adventures. He's Linda's opposite; he will impose his will on the world, he will make the grass and dust between trailers into the surface of the moon, and he'll be its conqueror. I do my best, at least for a while; we set up a little rocket with some chairs and I am the assistant pilot; we enact the blastoff; we veer and roar through space. He yells and falls down while I watch. Monsters interest me, and lost civilizations on other planets; but this is just action, pointless and dull. I have seen Zsa Zsa Gabor in *Queen of Outer Space*, in which she plays a Venusian queen who must remain masked because a nasty guy threw acid on her face. There are only women on her planet, and she likes it that way, though when a man shows up in a spaceship she is outraged in part because she is inflamed by desire, so she takes off the cat-eyed mask and reveals her disfigurement, and she makes him take off his shirt and tortures him until finally she gives in and kisses him and they escape together from Venus while the icy bitches of the planet all go up in flames.

No such fun with All Boy: Zoom, yell, fall, and soon I am bored out of my skull, and wind up sitting on the grass close to adults while they smoke and play cards and their laughter gets louder. But my evident restlessness draws the visit to an early close, something my mother doesn't really seem to mind. Safely out of the cluster of trailers, on the way home in our new Chevy Impala, she says, "I could *never* live in a trailer park." My father says, "Jimbo's a good old boy," his voice full of appreciation for his friend, and my mother doesn't answer.

❧

Nike Zeus, the missiles in the desert are called—shades of my book of archaeology! The engineers will work for years at fenced-off sites, and when they're done the holes with their projectiles aimed at Moscow will be covered over with earth and creosote and brush, only a little shack on the surface you'd never think contained an elevator, entrance to an underworld where two men sit in a control booth with a red telephone and a pair of key-operated red buttons.

My father's silo is called Site 9, and sometimes we go out there on weekends, when no one's working. My father has a security pass at the gate, so we can drive into the desert a ways from the site and have a cookout: T-bone steaks and watermelon. When my mother and I go for a picnic in the desert, as we do some days when I don't have school, it's different; we bring sandwiches, feed kangaroo rats, and watch cordons of ants go about the monumental labor of hauling away the potato chips we've laid out for them. But a cookout with my father is different. He brings along the new pistol he's bought, "for security," a black German Luger. He demonstrates how to put the chrome clip full of bullets in and pull it out, how to put the safety on, so the gun won't go off when you don't want it to. I line up cans and bottles from a sack we've brought along, and then he and my mother take turns at target practice. He tells her she must hold the pistol farther away from her eye; when she hits a can dead center he says, "That's my Ruthie, my girl's a wicked shot." We have a little fire and stay till just after sundown, when the desert hills cool and go blue. Detritus of our visit: shattered bottles, beer and soda cans shot full of holes, little bullet casings scattered in sand. There's a photo of the two of them by a campfire, the cooler bright in the foreground, intensely red in that odd desert evening light. Each with an arm around the other's waist. With his free hand he holds up a beer; in hers she brandishes the pistol. I must be the cameraman.

I do have a friendship with one boy, or something like a friendship. His name is Mikey, he lives two houses away, and although I like him he is retarded. My mother explains it's not his fault that he's different, that he doesn't understand what other children do, though I can sense even in her defense a certain disdain, which has to do with the fact that Mikey grunts. He looks just like all the rest of the neighborhood boys—tanned from playing outside, crew cut sun-bleached nearly white at the tips, old shorts and T-shirt, only a little dirtier than the rest of us—but he doesn't speak. Though he manages to express himself, if only for his own pleasure or satisfaction. I play with Mikey in the backyard, and he runs around grunting in the oleanders, a beast.

He is interesting for several reasons. First, he's almost infinitely pliable. You can play all sorts of games with him, put him in any position, and it's fine with him. You can say, Mikey, you are the mud puddle, and we are all going to jump in you and take a mudbath, and he just laughs and loves the whole thing. You can say, Mikey, you are the dog, now wear this collar and drink from a bowl, and he does and laughs and grunts some more.

Second, Mikey is always available. Other kids have homework and things to attend to, develop animosities, practice piano or the new social arts of rivalry and exclusivity, but not Mikey. He's around every minute, it seems, except when his mother calls him—"Mike-y, Mik-eey," over the gray cinder-block fences, the oleanders and tool sheds of the backyards. All you have to do is look at him, and he's right there next to you, your friend for life. Even if you don't deserve it.

Third, there is some sweetness about him, a contagious happiness that's hard to miss. Although of course it gets boring, the unmodulated pleasure, the fact that he's all dumb delight. If Linda would draw herself tiny, and Astro-Boy draw himself huge, filling the page with the force and singularity of himself, what would Mikey do? He's a blank screen, an open field, pure receptivity.

One day I have brought some scissors out of the house, and pretty soon I conceive a game of hairdresser, with Mikey as my client. He of course complies, holding still; I'm just going to give him the slightest trim, but before you know it I've botched it, there's a big chunk out of Mikey's already short hair. He looks like an accident victim, a fact not lost on his mother when he gets home.

That evening she shows up at our front door in a kind of quiet, contained rage. She and my mother talk in the living room, and I am called in. My mother asks if I have cut Mikey's hair, and I confess that I have, and Mikey's mother makes me a speech. She says, He likes you, he likes everyone, Mikey trusts you, he doesn't know what you know, he can't do the things you can do, and you don't have the right to treat him like that, you don't have the right to treat him like he's nothing and cut his hair. It's not all right to treat a friend like that.

I am so ashamed that I don't want to play with Mikey anymore, because I've done a bad thing. I've abused some power granted to me by accident. I don't see him much, so I'm startled, as my mother is, when Mikey and his mother ring our doorbell on Christmas Eve, and there he stands—hair grown back now into his stiff little brush cut—with a small package in his hand, a wrapped gift for me, a little yellow bulldozer, the sort of toy I'd never ask for myself but which I like: painted metal, detailed, with precisely turned wheels. Of course we don't have a present for Mikey—who'd have thought to? But Mikey's mother lets us know that's not the point, they just wanted to come and bring me a gift; Mikey wanted to give presents to his friends. Even then I can see what she's doing; it's not about me, she's working to make things normal for her son, so that he can do the things that children do on Christmas.

I like my second-grade teacher because she teaches us to make things; for Christmas we've done a bulletin board full of elaborate angels, their bodies tubes of rolled blue paper shaped like rockets, their wings fringed white, their hair sheeny white cotton brushed up and out. Is that how our souls will look in what my grandmother used to call "the next life," floating against the skyey backdrop of heaven? Now it's January, almost the end of the month, and we're making things about presidents: cherry trees and axes, log cabins. I am carrying home some such production one afternoon when there's a scene on East Twenty-second I've never seen before. There are police cars in the yard next door, and in our yard, and ambulances at Mikey's, crackly police radios, red lights twirling, and every now and then a siren letting out a little whoop as if it can't contain itself. People are standing around watching, the police officers keeping them at a distance, a big semicircle centered on Mikey's house, and now the neighbors are being interviewed, because Mikey's father has taken a gun and shot Mikey, and his other son, and his wife, and himself.

That boy I was, clutch of school papers in hand, seems unable to take in these events, or rather, all he can do is take them in, all eyes and ears, a kind of recording instrument unable to interpret. Like a lunar vehicle, one of those probes which will be sent out, in a few years, onto the surface of the moon, the sort that thinks nothing, assesses nothing, merely collects. Bits and pieces of perception—neighbors standing and talking, the bits of overheard talk, the police radios fierce with staticky voices like broadcasts from satellites, something in the newspaper the next day, on the TV news? Maybe he hears his parents talking about it, in the kitchen, when he's not supposed to hear? Something about no money, about how hard it is to have a child who's not all right, the pain of a boy with something wrong with him?

Strange sense of a wound in the neighborhood, the continuity ripped. Once opened, the gap persists. Everybody gone. Mikey's house empty, yard full of tumbleweeds.

Thirty-seven years later I'll have dinner with my father in a Tucson steakhouse, and we'll set to reminiscing about East Twenty-second Street, that raw, dusty corridor where the wind pushed the tumbleweeds down the middle of the street. He'll say, "Remember when that woman killed her family?" And I'll say, "Wasn't it the father? I remember it as the father," but in fact I've got it wrong. And maybe that's why I can't remember the reaction of the boy I was to the erasure of a family, to the detonation of a parent's rage: I wasn't paying attention, exactly, to the facts of the story; I was revising it into something I could bear.

5

Firebird

My mother's taking art lessons at Helen Doyle's Hacienda Bellas Artes. The Hacienda's an arched, fired-adobe manor in the desert east of town, every room elevated by Mrs. Doyle's handiwork; she glazed these geometric floor tiles set into the steps, and worked the mosaic in a niche in the room devoted to yarn; she forged these heavy wrought-iron gates that cover the glass doors of the gallery, my favorite room, cool, terrazzoed, usually closed, its walls hung with Mrs. Doyle's important paintings. Here's a cubistic rendering of three musicians, their fragmented cello and violins rendered in bronze and dull blues, for which she won a prize of several thousand dollars; here some Western landscapes of blue mountains and spiky palo verde trees in their yellowy spring green. Here, best of all, a painting both elegant and disturbing: a portrait of Mrs. Doyle's daughter, in a low-cut yellow dress from which her long pale neck rises to the white oval of her face, which is topped by ringlets and a loopy-looking yellow hat, a Regency affair crowned with white ostrich plumes. Beside the elongated young woman is an equally stretched-out Afghan hound; heads turned at the same angle, three-quarter profile, woman and dog both display large, nervous eyes.

I don't know what's become of the daughter, but the skittish Afghan or its descendant is with us still; Mrs. Doyle has to keep the wooden gate that leads from the garden to stairs up to the flat roof latched, or otherwise, she says, the dog will run up and attempt to fling itself from the top of the house. Encounters with the beast—a Modigliani dog animated by Disney—confirm that it really is both shockingly elongated and suicidally nervous.

My mother goes to painting class—in groups sometimes, occasionally for a private lesson—several times a week. I've never before known her to pick up a pencil to sketch, never seen her with a box of paints, and suddenly we have irresistible boxes of opaque watercolors in tubes, blocks of textured paper, luscious-smelling linseed oil and turpentine, and more and more oils added to her wooden box: fat tubes of Titanium White, slender ones of Burnt Sienna, Cobalt, and my favorite name: Fugitive Lake.

In my mind, at least, there is some link between this sudden flowering of desire to fill page and canvas with form and color, and my mother's new love, which is the desert itself: shift of light and shadow, blue and gold, the soft austerity of arroyo and foothill and mountain. The desert is sparse and intensely alive at once. Suddenly this vivid place, for which she has no precedent, has won her allegiance; for the first time she seems to have found a landscape that speaks to her deeply, that is in some inexplicable way *hers*. When you love a place enough, it seems almost to be inside you, as if it were the physical equivalent of an inner life.

And we've moved to a new house, on Priscilla Avenue, in a new development on the edge of town. It's another world from the cinderblock and sandstorm grit of East Twenty-second Street, those squat houses painted yellow and pale green, tricycles and bikes tangled in the front yards, tumbleweeds and trash caught in chain-link fences. These houses have floor-to-ceiling strips of window that face the street, and the living rooms sport "cathedral ceilings," a rather grand term for a space that does in fact feel lofty to us, a peaked room banded on the southern side with clerestory windows we fill with pieces of colored glass. "Cathedral" suits the house, for me, because from the back yard, where our plot of dry land surrounded by a fence of woven metal slats faces endless acres of desert, you can look right up into the smoke-blue heaven of the Santa Catalina mountains, where one notched peak looms, twin spires of rock in its cleft forming a cathedral infinitely more grand than our ceiling. I study it through my father's binoculars.

The house fills up with the new evidence of my mother's creativity: stiff watercolors first, then increasingly confident oils. She looks darker, the result of hours out in the foothills, in the stony lower reaches of the canyons, painting, and it's as if she's letting the colors of the place into her, her skin grown ocher, her hair stone-black and lustrous, and she takes to wearing silver bracelets, some of them studded with turquoise. What seemed strained in her, closed, opens out, as if all that air and light unclenched her. It's a lesson, still, how a landscape in which you have faith, with which you are able to become entranced, can open and change a life. What transforms us like the experience of enchantment?

It's also the first time I've known my mother to have a friend—and a startlingly different one at that. Mrs. Doyle is the closest thing to a bohemian to have appeared in my mother's life; she wears muumuus in tropical prints of hibiscus and bird of paradise outlined in gold; she found them at Kresge's for $2.99, bought six of them, and wears them to polish her Byzantine icons. She wears a heavy necklace of old Navajo silver, hammered squash blossoms, and half-round glasses on a knotted silk cord around her neck so that they bounce just above the slight, rounded protuberance of her belly. Helen Doyle's life is clearly organized not around her children, or her husband, or running the household. Mr. Doyle, happily retired from his paint business, is largely invisible, puttering around sheds or the desert in pink-and-green pants Mrs. Doyle has purchased for him. She is an instance of a life given over to an entirely different set of needs than those which have shaped us so far, and she fascinates both me and my mother, though there is always that bit of inequality in their friendship brought about by the fact that my mother is the student and Helen the teacher. Like many a self-made artist, one who has willed herself into being, there is a bit of the prima donna about her: "Diego always used to say to me . . ." she liked to say, or "Nothing speaks to me with the force of the Byzantine."

Though she did indeed study with Diego Rivera, taking little planes down to Mexico City "in the days when the stewardess would just give you a stick of gum and say 'Good luck,'" her important paintings have hung on the gallery walls for years, unsold. She likes to disparage Ted deGrazia, a schlocky but very successful painter who's made a career of sentimental renderings of faceless little Indian children done up as angels. "I taught him to paint," she'd wail, "and then he turns out shit and makes a fortune!" Mr. Doyle's retirement income is not quite adequate to her plans: thus the yarn shop, the group lessons in still life. Mrs. Doyle feels the new developments—like ours—are cutting too deeply into the desert, moving too close to her. So she wishes to build another house, on the other side of town, out in an area of old orange and date-palm groves. She's designed a neo-Arabian villa, with a dome for meditation, its plaster pierced with little shapes of brilliantly colored glass in cobalt and very deep red.

My mother drives out to visit Helen sometimes even on days when they haven't scheduled lessons. The two will have tea and snacks on pottery dishes Helen's made, some of which have been molded on real melons, then glazed black on the outside, lustrous coral within: "So Russian!" Helen exclaims.

∽

About this time a sort of cultural juggernaut began, which had as its goal the betterment of me, so that I would later enjoy the benefits of a firm grounding in the finer stuff of the educated life. My parents ordered (from a TV ad?) the Reader's Digest Collection of 100 Great Masterpieces of World Music (*order now and you'll also receive . . .*). It didn't matter that the box of records that came were in fact a compilation of snippets, the most famous bits from this and that. We'd listen to them and learn to recognize the bits; we'd make a game of it: How quickly can you name this piece of music, and the composer? Dance of the Hours from La Gioconda! By? By . . . um . . . Ponchielli!

This was fun, but not as compelling to me as the visual component of my new aesthetic education, which consisted of boxed sets of slides from the Louvre and the National Gallery. We had just the information on the bottom of the slide, and the date: Michelangelo Merisi, known as Caravaggio, circa 1603. My cultural imprinting and my mother's study of oil painting were thus furthered at once. And though we also used them for a kind of memory drill (This bathing Venus? Rubens!), an education in style was being conveyed, some sense of the wildly various lenses through which the world might be seen. Like the way the optometrist had worked, fitting me for my new glasses, in their "smoked plastic" frames; *which do you like better, A or B? Now which is clearer?* Here was a universe of renderings, from smooth Madonnas, their skin glazed to an unmarred translucence, to the spiky dappled pinwheels of Van Gogh.

(My new glasses came shortly after my new bicycle, and my bicycle accident. My father had taken me to the playground of Whetmore Elementary to practice riding the new bike. I'd loved the feeling of speed, coming down the long dusty slope, but I didn't quite understand how the brakes worked, and couldn't really see the high chain-link fence and the galvanized metal post that was hurrying right toward my left eye. An hour after the collision I had a huge lump just at the top of my eye socket, which shrank into a shiner of increasingly artful hues, as black and blue green as my old bread molds had been. My third-grade teacher, whose name has disappeared in a fog like the one I used to see from the back of the room when she wrote on the chalkboard, pointed out that I seemed to be squinting a good deal anyway. Soon I was outfitted with a bookish-looking new pair of spectacles that brought the world into a startling focus. I'd assumed everyone saw the same soft-focus blur I did, the world by Monet. The bicycle was returned to the store, a similar strategy to the one my parents had chosen when my first dog died; I was so hopelessly grief-stricken it was ruled I should never have a dog again. It would take me thirty more years to acquire a bicycle and a puppy, and to discover that these constituted two of my chief pleasures.)

Suddenly sharper, newly bold in their outlines, the images on our living room wall taught me more than style. They were vessels of something beyond themselves; their subtle, potent work was the transmission of world and culture despite a historical void around them, despite an absence of assigned meanings. It almost didn't matter; all by themselves, projected on the living room wall, onto the new white Sheetrock, they meant, and meant intensely. Here were Circumcisions (which my mother found distasteful) and Salomes, Davids, Judiths with the sad and grisly heads of Holofernes; here were Floras and Psyches, and allegories of Time, and soap bubbles caught forever in virtuoso demonstrations of technique; here were the hushed rooms of Vermeer, like Helen Doyle's gallery. Here was evidence both antique and new: when we looked at the title of Caravaggio's image, that geisha-haired boy with the full-lipped pout, his delicate fingers toying with a dish of cleft and dewy fruit, my father said, "That's a boy?"

Sometimes at the end of the box we'd start over again, and look till we were too tired, our eyes too full for any more, after we'd been talking about the pictures all evening. And so what may have begun in naïveté ended in grace; the music and the pictures entered us, drew us into their sphere of time and of style, and drew us together. We wouldn't ever be this much of a family again, this much in easy relation, though of course we didn't know that.

~

My studies in art history bore an immediate and surprising result in school, in the classroom of my new fourth-grade teacher, Miss Tynes, a tall woman with a loose red swathe of hair piled high on her head in Gibson girl fashion, and a fine clutches of soft lines around her eyes. She wore beautiful and subtly colored shawls she'd woven of mohair and alpaca, yarns whose names I loved to learn, words nearly as tactile as what they signified. Often the shawl was secured by a big silver pin, something sculptural, centered on a lozenge of obsidian or a tear of jade. Miss Tynes believed in our education in the arts, which is to say that she was devoted to the cultivation of our spirits. She approached her work in a seamless and coherent fashion I now recognize as evidence of a sort of commitment I'd never before seen anyone muster for anything, not quite.

Our first evidence of this faith, of her unusual predilection, was also my opportunity to shine. Miss Tynes announced, early in the school year (our pencil boxes still new, tablets blank, the prospect of order tantalizing, still possible) that our class belonged to a club, the Object of the Month Club, which was sponsored by the Metropolitan Museum in New York City, a huge building which held some of the great treasures of the world. Each month we would receive a copy of a different work of art, and each time it would be something surprising, probably something we'd never seen before. On an easel beside her rested a framed canvas, its blank backside turned to us, and when she lifted it and turned it around, there was a familiar, soft-focus image, a pink-cheeked blond girl in a black outfit standing on a garden path, both arms holding up a gardener's watering can.

Miss Tynes said, "Does anyone know the name of this painting, or the name of the artist who painted it?"

I raise my hand, am called upon, and announce, "That is *Girl with a Watering Can*, by Pierre-Auguste Renoir."

The "Pierre-Auguste" part is, of course, the flourish on my bit of knowledge that begins a relationship between Miss Tynes and me that is collaborative, thrilling, collegial; I am a special boy, I am athirst for the sort of knowledge that flows from her so easily, an acolyte in her church. She recognizes me in some way that is new for me.

Miss Tynes is a weaver; her looms, her enchantment with fiber, are the center of her life, and she has even shown her work, she tells my mother, at the DeYoung Museum in Golden Gate Park in San Francisco, a collection of names that sound to me as burnished and evocative of other worlds as, say, Dar-es-Salaam. Under Miss Tynes's tutelage—lucky for me she has to teach to earn a living; what's a weaver to do, in 1962?—my love of exotic places flowers. I am a connoisseur of places I can't go. I read Edgar Rice Burroughs's *Tarzan and the Jewels of Opar* and daydream about that lost city, unreachable on its vined escarpment—Opar, whose name echoes the opal my mother's bought in Mexico, a "fire opal" with gleams of brilliant orange leaping out of deep facets inside the smooth body of the stone. Sometimes I am enthralled by books of a deep sadness: the cruel struggles of *Black Beauty*, the unwavering devotion of *Old Yeller*, and a novel about a cougar who lives high on a cliff in the desert mountains, singular, golden-eyed, heartbreakingly alone. I read a book by Richard Halliburton about Tibet, the Kingdom at the Roof of the World, and love to imagine the towers, the scented pavilions occupied, sometimes, by clouds. Nepal, Golden Gate Park: glimmering openings toward other, hidden chambers of the world.

Chambers Miss Tynes herself opens. She provides us with large, fragrant hunks of wet terra-cotta clay, and later with Conté crayons in a matching color. She produces from a cabinet Japanese brushes and inks and explains the patterns of haiku. We dig abstract and tunneled forms in the playground dirt, fill them with wet plaster of Paris we've mixed with sawdust for strength, then clean away the soil with toothbrushes and whisks, junior archaeologists, to reveal the sculptural forms we've cast. We commence a project, burlap stitchery, each of us given a large piece of scratchy, fragrant brown cloth. We fringe the edges, then dig into her vast stock of yarn scraps, everything from fat pieces of early-sixties Day-Glo to twined silks, striated cottons, shimmery flosses, wools wound in gold like the poles on the docks of Venice. The yarns, her accumulated wastes and trimmings, comprise a lexicon of texture, an encyclopedia of shadings and variations, a dazzling multiplicity. We're issued broad, blunt-tipped embroidery needles and set to, choosing our favorite scraps to thread through the needles' eyes and the holes in the weave of the burlap.

I begin an intricate, free-form design, spirals and shapes spilling into one another. I stitch a pink spiral, like a nautilus shell, the whorl of a snail, with ribs of violet, and a yellow-and-green explosion beside it; the result is abstract but refers to natural forms. I love this; I lose myself in it, in the hues and heft of the wool between my fingers, the earthy burlap, the satisfying regularity of the movement of the needle. I pour out of myself into the work.

Our creations are called stitcheries, not embroidery, my teacher explains, since embroidery is a craft usually executed by following a pattern someone else has determined. The worst thing is to follow someone else's design. One day I collaborate with another kid on an evil drawing of Kevin, a boy we all tease because he's weird, and is said to pick his nose and eat what he discovers. This may or may not be true, but I am grateful that someone is plainly weirder than me, and I participate in the group project to torment him. My friend Walter and I make a sketch of Kevin, with horns coming out of his head; we picture him peeing into a cup. To my mortification Miss Tynes spies the drawing, but she has also just discovered that some girls are using tracing paper to copy pictures from a coloring book. This practice appalls her, and she proclaims that our drawing of Kevin is more creative, and promptly pins it up on the bulletin board. *You are the maker of your design,* she says. *Copies are lifeless but your own designs are aglow with life.* I'm ashamed, and in a while I sneak my hateful picture down from the wall, but the message runs deeper than embarrassment.

We are allowed to take our stitcheries-in-progress home, if we choose, and I do, so that I can continue my contemplative work. My mother admires it but doesn't know what it represents; I tell her I see my design as a kind of sky. She suggests that I consider switching to a landscape: sky over the desert mountains, saguaros. I add a saguaro in green floss, its twin arms happily poking up at heaven, and take it to school next day, but Miss Tynes is disappointed. *Why restrict yourself to the limitations of tired representation,* she suggests, in some other words which are lost to me now, *when you have the whole spectrum of this luscious stuff to play with? The yarns themselves can tell you what to do; who needs the stiff strictures of material reality to define the province of art?*

Object of the month: a swirling jimsonweed by Georgia O'Keeffe, like a petticoat on a laundry line, filmy nylon in a slow whirlwind. I cover my saguaro over with swirls and drifts, paisley shapes, rippled and dotted intricacies of silk.

I like this activity so much I would do it all day, and Miss Tynes is complicitous in my dereliction of other things, especially PE. I hate PE, though it's only playing kickball with a soft rubber ball. I hate kickball, hate especially the big ball, which is the color of wet terra-cotta clay, and which yields a little when you kick it, making a kind of hollow sound with an echo inside it, like a stomach being punched. It smells rubbery, unhappy, closeted, like the smell of the safety patrol's cloakroom. It smells of inadequacy, not knowing what to do, not knowing how. Some days PE consists of relay races or a running game. Already I am a chubby boy; I wear Husky Boy jeans from Sears, the label loudly identifying my category. And I don't seem to know the rules to anything (except the intricacies of hopscotch, to which I have paid attention, and the elaborate procedures of jump rope, a girls' province I occasionally visit, as a boy who's viewed as an unthreatening if not always welcome visitor from the other side. I have even smuggled *Little Women* out of the school library, because the girls have spoken so excitedly of the nobility of Jo and the tragedy of Beth, and somehow I know it's something I shouldn't be seen actually checking out). When it's PE time, I linger behind or slip to the back of the line, and from thence flit into the shadows under the metal-and-concrete steps that march from Whetmore Elementary onto the playground. I bring my stitchery with me and work on through the period, or I read *Myths and Legends of the Inca*: condors, golden masks, ruined cities. The burlap in my lap smells fibery, alive—vaguely redolent of some tropical place, something carried in the hold of a ship, exotic fruit, coffee, roots from the equator. I would like to go to Peru, to Machu Picchu. I have been imagining its high sorrow and dignity, the sun rising on that empty fortress and no one there at all but the stones with their mute knowledge of time, and the black arcs of eagles high over it all, over what is already impossibly high, dizzyingly up above us all. I've seen a movie on TV one afternoon (when the best old ones are on) when I was home with a sore throat. This one starred Yma Sumac, who played an Inca princess who sang hymns to the sun in an incredible voice that spiraled octaves up and up like the condors I imagined, until she offended somebody and got thrown into a volcano at the end. I feel the wild, high reaches of her throbbing coloratura in my own scratchy throat. If a voice could rise out of sight it would sound like hers.

Of course Miss Tynes knows just what I am doing; looking back toward me from the playing field where she is refereeing the kickball game, does she think she really ought to come and get me? If so, she never does, though she tells my mother, who also doesn't seem to mind.

Miss Tynes teaches us everything, except for Spanish, which takes place in another room, down the hall, where the vivacious Señorita Fernandez teaches us to count, sing, and engage in charmingly stilted conversations: *Como estás, Marcos? Muy bien, Señorita Fernandez, como está usted?* Every other field of enquiry is the desmesne of Miss Tynes. She makes no secret of her dislike for math, which I don't care for either; we get through it dutifully. Science is better, since it lends itself, at least in her hands, to the investigation of materials, the splendid stuff out of which we might *make*. For my Science Fair project I mount a study of natural dyes; I collect leaves and bark from the desert, boil them until they yield their colors, dip spun wool into the tinctures, add a fixative, and *voilà!*—earthy little samples of yarns in a palette of desert shades, pale sienna, russety purple (from onion peels), yellows and sage greens. I mount them on a large poster, and win a ribbon, some consolation to my mother, in whose saucepans I've been stewing foul-smelling concoctions of creosote and bear claw, cholla and mesquite. My dyes are the sort native peoples might have used, though I don't, like them, use urine as a mordant, interested as I am in the idea.

We talk, in class, about native peoples. Miss Tynes brings in a weighty necklace of Navajo silver, a garland of sculptural pomegranate blossoms. She spins yarn with a Navajo spinning wheel, a single stick with a little wooden disk partway up its length, pulling the hunk of carded wool away with one hand, using the other to spin the stick and catch and twist the long fibers, turning an amorphous cloud into a winding ball of thread. She brings to school—in a wrapping of cloth—a mysterious roll of Indian flatbread, an astonishingly thin grayish product you can see through, its color and texture not unlike the glassine envelopes in which I've been buying stamps for my new collection. The bread, she tells us, lasts forever in the desert air; rolls of the bread, like this one, have been found in the ancient dwellings, perfectly preserved, ready to nourish.

∾

Object of the Month, this one unveiled with ceremony. It has arrived in a square, varnished pine box, sealed with heavy metal latches. Different children volunteer to open each closure, then one girl (lucky!) lifts the wooden lid away. Inside is the mummy of an Egyptian cat, or rather the bronze casing of such a mummy, poised, sleekly muscled, its gaze perfectly straightforward, its one golden earring flashing. Walter and I love the cat. Walter is my best friend in the class, a slight, underfed boy with narrow features and a dark crew cut; he is a wiry and wiggly boy, not like me at all, but we both like to take advantage of a special privilege: when we have finished our work and others are still busy, we are allowed to go to the back of the room and visit the cat. We study it, and the hieroglyphics carved at its base.

Walter and I are Cub Scouts, and one day a week we wear our uniforms to school, navy blue outfits with jaunty yellow scarves secured by brass holders like napkin rings emblazoned with the faces of wolves or bears. My mother, returning to the social mode of her Eastern Star days, has become a den mother, organizing the weekly activities of some dozen little boys. Since this outgoing, administrative position goes against her essentially introverted nature, some signs of strain are evident, but she treats our Cub Scout troop as guests and is a flawless hostess. We pursue a project in the backyard, at picnic tables, and she emerges with trays of little sandwiches cut into triangles, and pitchers of lemonade, exuding a combination of warmth and effortlessness, projecting the sense that nothing in the world is more important to her than the immediate needs of ten-year-old boys. Thus other kids think my mother is wonderful, which I appreciate while noting nonetheless the difference between the vivacity with which she greets the scouts and the plainer life of every day. At scout meetings she is efficient, carefree, modern in her jeans and Western shirts, the picture of organization, even though I know some of our activities are a trial to her. All Cub Scouts in Tucson, for instance, are required to construct a rocket of balsa wood, and we must travel to a big metal building where hundreds of uniformed boys race their creations, which zip along on wires strung in the air: ho-hum. We both prefer the Blue and Gold Banquet, an event held in my school cafeteria, at which scouts perform and receive badges and awards. I like the rarefied atmosphere the name suggests; the romance of azure and gold, the medieval ring of *banquet*. My mother glazes hams, securing pineapple rings to their scored surfaces with whole cloves. Does she work so hard as a den mother because she wants me to befriend other boys? At the banquet—dressed in a sequined sombrero and a serape, holding a guitar I can't play—I perform in Spanish, singing a cappella a song I've learned from a record:

Estas son las manzanitas
En el jardín de David. . . .

I receive enthusiastic applause.

The troop does yield a raft of friends: first, Kurt, who teaches me dirty words and the uses of pocketknives. I buy my first one, a beauty, at the new Circle K on Craycroft Road; a little silver horse's head floats dreamily on a black field, so deep inside layers of clear lacquer he could never be touched. When I lose it in the arroyo, it isn't the knife itself but that chrome profile, mane forever lifted in the wind, that occasions a minor heartbreak. Then there's Tony Dallesandro, who has an immense collection of little plastic figures of men: soldiers, cowboys, Indians who must always die and die again. The Dallesandros live in a big house in the desert, an atmospheric adobe like Hacienda Bellas Artes, and my mother likes to go for a visit so I can play with Tony while she and Mrs. Dallesandro have coffee; it is a social step up, though there's a sense that the Dallesandros are to be admired from a distance, elevated somehow just out of our reach. It isn't only the nice big house. Everyone seems fascinated by Tony's beauty, which even my father remarks on: he's a little Tadzio, with curly bronze hair and huge brown eyes, his eyelashes of an unnatural length and curl. He seems to have stepped from one of our slides, a Renaissance allegory of perfected boyhood, though he zooms around his room entirely engaged in the defeat and toppling of hundreds of plastic men.

Some days after school I go to Walter's house; we've invented a game we play in his room, with the door closed. It goes like this: because Walter is my baby, he must take off his shirt and sit in my lap. He keeps his blue jeans on. My baby cries and needs his belly rubbed, needs me to stroke his chest and the brushy stubble of his head to soothe him. That's all there is to it; when the baby feels better he stops crying and doesn't need to be stroked, but in a moment he'll be upset again. I love this game, and in some way Walter's body partakes of some aspect of the Egyptian cat: his leanness, the sculptural muscle of his little chest and belly. Walter isn't pretty like Tony, but he's available, and there is something entirely compelling in his small, solid curves. Why do we always close his door? Because we know we're pursuing some mystery? Something to be translated, like the hieroglyphics?

～

Memphis seems a lost world now, made strange by our absence from it, so remote it might as well really be in Egypt. My mother and I visit once, on the train, an adventure alternately dreamy and boring; the black tracks seem to cross the desert forever. In little Southern towns, people sell box lunches from the platforms, and I'm allowed to lean out the window and give a lady a dollar for a white paper box containing a piece of fried chicken and a delicious buttery biscuit. We see Sally's new baby, her third, and we move in a world I barely recognize. At Christmas Sally sends elaborately wrapped gifts: airy white divinity she's made herself, all melting white sugar and big pecans; Avon sachets; jewelry for my mother from Sarah Coventry, a special sparkling ornament tied to each bow. The presents are beautiful; she wants to please. Her gesture seems to come from very far away.

～

My junior sexual investigations are not limited to lithe Walter. I have also entered into a secret liaison with a neighbor girl, Lorraine Gunther, who is a rather Juno-esque thirteen. Lorraine (pointedly pronounced *LORR-aine*, not *Lorr-AINE*) has invented a name for our game, Sneak Previews, which even then strikes me as a bit smarmy. She's taken pleasure in telling her mother that we play Sneak Previews, which she explained is a game in which we tell each other the plots of new movies we have heard about. This explanation is obviously inadequate for the frequency with which our sessions are scheduled.

Mrs. Gunther belongs to one of two new categories of adults I have recently learned from my parents. She is a *divorcée*, which is a descriptive term plainly offered as a judgment, though what is described or judged, exactly, I can't tell. Thus the term connotes things specific to Mrs. Gunther: arched eyebrows drawn in pencil, pedal-pusher pants, a collection of Chesty Morgan albums. (My other new category is *spinster*, a niche occupied by Beulah across the street, who drives an elaborate pink-and-gray Buick and has, in her stale and doilied living room, porcelain figurines of shepherdesses. Beulah, my parents suggest, is prissy and overly fussy because she has not had a man; Mrs. Gunther demonstrates the results of having had too many.)

Sneak Previews is conducted at the Gunthers' when the divorcée is not at home, or at my house when my mother is at painting class. We usually go into the closet anyway, for added safety or drama. Lorraine, who is in junior high and goes to Catholic school, something which is a complete mystery to me, removes one article of her clothing at a time, as do I sometimes: the game is more about her nakedness than mine. Her breasts are large, with big dark brown nipples like my mother's; her body is very white and between her legs is a dark triangle of hair I don't think pretty.

(Here some half memory—no, some smaller fraction—both wavers and insists at once. Did this happen? I'm a little boy, taking a bath with my mother, sitting between her legs in water opaque with soap. It's hot, and everything feels too close. Something about her body—heaviness of the breasts, that dark hair wet between her thighs, something uneasy, as if it's not safe to be there. Did *what* happen? The little piece of film sputters, replays: that's all there is. The memory movie makes me feel a little sick. How is it to be understood? The mother frightened the boy with her touch, which he now cannot remember? The boy became frightened of the physicality of the mother's body, because he understood that he loved his mother but did not love women's bodies, and suddenly felt lost in this contradiction? Or frightened because his mother *was* a body, a thickening body, and his little form would slip away between her legs, into the future, while hers fell backward, into time, away from him?)

The secret allure of our game, for me, is that it is not entirely pleasant; a little *frisson* created by the mixture of interest and of repulsion makes it fascinate. One day we must feel extra safe from intrusion, since we emerge from the closet in my room. I am naked and have a nine-year-old's version of an erection, and I strut around like a proud little prince, to Lorraine's delight. She lies on the bed and instructs me to place the eraser end of a pencil in her vagina, which I do: odd little folds and crevices, moist and unfamiliar. I am instructed to sniff the pencil, and taste it, which I do, and we collapse in laughter. Later I have the distinct sense that my mother knows what's up—not the shocking action with the pencil,

77

Firebird

specifically, but the nature of our recurrent game. But as with my hiding out from PE, nothing's said. Perhaps my investigation of the opposite sex comes as a sort of relief?

∾

I have seen my parents making love. I've come home from somewhere, earlier than they'd expected me. I look around but don't see them, I have something to ask or tell them, where are they? Their bedroom door is shut but it doesn't stop me, I turn the knob and open it just partway before I see: my mother's darker body beneath my father's pale pink and white one, his buttocks pumping up and down, though as soon as he hears the knob he's already turning his head over his shoulder to look, making a noise of surprise at being discovered, pulling out of her. I close the door and hurry away; I don't know what to do, go to the kitchen for a glass of water? Soon my mother hurries out of their room in her nightgown, closing the door behind her. She comes to me so solicitously, with such grave concern that it is clear I've seen something for which I need to be consoled.

∾

Our class is going to the symphony! All the fourth-grade classes in the city will travel by bus to the university, to Symphony Hall, and the orchestra will offer a program of symphonic music. We are lucky to know the selections ahead of time, so we can understand the beauty and nuance of what we will hear. We study the components of an orchestra, we discuss appropriate behavior (especially the necessity of attentive silence, and the need to discern when a piece is actually *over*, since the worst thing is to clap between movements, an embarrassment to all concerned).

We will hear Smetana's *The Bartered Bride* and Manuel de Falla's *El Amor brujo*, a ballet score about a Spanish sorcerer and Gypsy passion, whose title conjures for me the label of a cologne my mother always wears, a black mantilla and a clutch of blooms printed beneath the words *Flor de Blas*. She's bought a black mantilla herself, and for special occasions pins it in her hair, dons a jingling trio of thin silver bracelets, fastens a gardenia to her collar and enters my room on a cloud of Flor de Blas, underpinned by the duskier scent of the gardenia, to kiss me good night because they are going . . . Where on earth are they going? A party for the men who work at the missile sites, dinner in a fancy Mexican restaurant? Everyone is proud that I do not require a baby-sitter; I like to be home alone: there is reading, there are Tarzan movies on TV, or badly dubbed Italian movies about Hercules, always the same: a hero, a princess, a tiresome comic dwarf. At some point Hercules will be tortured, which is the best part: strapped to a table or tied to a tree, oiled and naked but for a loincloth or a short white pleated skirt, the hero will ripple and writhe. The best part of *El Amor brujo* is called "Ritual Fire Dance," a sexy appellation redolent of Hercules or Yma Sumac.

I have discovered masturbation, or at least a prepubescent version thereof. My parents have a back massager, a black contraption with a red rubber tip shaped like a suction cup; plug it in and switch it on and the cup vibrates back and forth so rapidly you can't really see it move, just a blur at the tip. They keep it in their bedside table, in a drawer beneath the alarm clock with its glowing radium dial and its frame of blue-tinted mirror glass. When they're gone I go and get it, plug in the long black cord, and then hold the head of it in my lap, right up against myself; the vibration, through the cloth of my pants, produces an irresistible pleasure, the perfect accompaniment to the travails of Hercules. This delight ends in a crescendo suddenly almost too intense to stand then turns to pain: Ritual Fire Dance. I'm too young for an ejaculation, but something's happened, a peak and culmination. Now hide it, quick, put it back in exactly the position you found it.

Crescendo: new word I've learned in relation to my favorite of the symphonic pieces we will hear, the *Suite from the Firebird* by Igor Stravinsky. Miss Tynes plays a recording of the suite while we paint with watercolors on slick, wet paper, making swirling impressions of the music on the page. I love this; my brush moves in bolder gestures of delight while the music mounts its fanfares, its repeated waves of triumphant flourish. When the paint's barely dry, I take a small brush and India ink and commence to sketch, atop my swirl of colors, each instrument and its player, little stick musicians all in motion, their bodies full of the rhythms of that fanfare, visible music pouring from cello and horn. Miss Tynes is mad for my drawing; it is my finest work, because I have gone inside the experience of the music, I have drawn the way the music feels.

Another day it is time to experience the music in another way, with all of our bodies. All the desks in the classroom are pushed to the perimeter, creating an open space in the center in which we all stand. Miss Tynes tells us the story of the firebird, how that phoenix immolates itself and dances in the flames, and then rises up again, radiant and new in the veils of its own ashes. We are to close our eyes, and then the music will begin. When we are ready, when we feel the music within us, then we may begin to move. We wait in our self-made dark. Crackle at the beginning of the record, then silence, and then the firebird's opening strains: something approaching, like weather. We're still at first, but then a few kids begin to sway, and then to rock, and soon we are stepping and turning, turning every which way, in a freedom of motion which, in truth, I myself have instigated, because I am suddenly deeply at home in the music, which seems to inhabit me, and as the piece mounts in intensity so does my movement, the fluidity of my arms in their ripples and archings, the bowing of my legs, the bending of my spine. At first I must be careful not to bump into them, but soon they've become invisible to me, the other children; there isn't any classroom around me anymore; the music is effortless grace and, subsumed by it, I also am effortless, something written quickly in the air. I'm utterly transported, and free, and weightless as the slides projected on our living room walls. Haven't I always been fire, and never known it?

Miss Tynes is, I think, flabbergasted—or at least I imagine so now. Who is this boy who pirouettes in his Husky Boy jeans as if he hadn't a shred of shame? At the time it seemed to me so matter-of-fact: who wouldn't give themselves over to such an outpouring, who wouldn't let that music come welling up as if it came not out of our portable phonograph but from the depths of the body? That is what has fallen away, like the firebird's scorched and immolated veil: my shame. How could I even know I carried it, until I laid it down?

She *must* think this scene something of a marvel, because she institutes this plan: the next day she invites me to perform an improvisational dance to the music again, but this time alone. The other children will sit at the desks pushed to the rim of the room; they can watch if they like, or sketch or read: *Today Mark is going to dance for us.* They don't seem to matter right now, to her or to me, and in fact I erase them, I accept the invitation without hesitation. Of course I will dance again, and this time in an open space, without the distracting hazard of other dancers.

I'm alone in the center of the room, and of course the lights don't change but in my memory they do, the edges gone shadowy while I stand at the heart of a circle of light. Opening swell of the strings, looming on the horizon, waver of the firebird's theme, little glimmers of light in the depths of the forest, scents of sandalwood and fragrant roots. Mad skitter of violins, and I am lifted, all sudden speed and purpose; I am *l'oiseau de feu*; nothing in my body holds me in place. If the other children watch, what do they think, do they think of me at all? Do they find me a little ridiculous, heavy little sissy in glasses and a plaid short-sleeved shirt? No idea. Miss Tynes watches, and appreciates, but even she is receding into the dark ring which surrounds this space in which I am coming to live.

Everything recedes into that twilight round: I won't remember the concert itself, but this moment, the music brilliant, this moment singular and bright in memory as some Russian gem. Here is the Princesses' Round, all sway and respite, elegance and reserve. But out of nowhere comes a walloping burst, kettle drum and horn, the Dance of the King; spinning on the axis of one leg, the other kicking at whatever would restrain me, I am power and authority. One arm up and one down, switch again, every muscle animated by what travels through me; now I've disappeared, now I've put myself entirely into someone else's hands; not my will but will itself is what courses through me. There's that skittering bird again, the hurry of his heated wings, and my ferocity quiets to lullaby, croon, and pulse, I'm on my knees and swaying, a gnarled shape, a root, and Oriental smokes drift slowly up from the towers, the minarets and onion domes decorating the lid of a black lacquer box. Everything quietens, everything's diminished, till—there, you hear it, what is this that has been granted us, what is this purity and force emerging in the horns? It is the firebird after all, no longer a hide-and-seek flitting in the trees but who he always was, beneath the scorch and the ashes, beneath the ordinary ugly body in which he has been disguised, under the shame he's worn like a cloak, under the misunderstandings and the knowledge that he can't be who they want, that they do not want who he is.

Here is who he is, swelling, taking form, the real body, triumphant boy, the bird in the fullness of its light, larger, empowered. Isn't it fire itself, the fact of burning, which enables the bird to dance? Then swirling around him the gorgeous cloaks, the brassy fabric of trumpets, the facades and the fanfares glorious, above them all. And rising, higher, the tower of light the bird is entering, which is the calmly flaming elevation of his own body, transfigured to something we can barely see—but given, here, sound.

And so we're left with shimmer and the downward drift of a minor chord, darkening, and then the emphatic burst of conclusion. Unsayable movement, given form, in the body of a heavy little boy no longer weighted, without limit, hardly held to earth at all.

6

Seventy-six Trombones

We have moved to Titusville, Florida, and I am enrolled in Miss Stephanie's School of the Dance. Months ago, back in Tucson, my parents told me I would be able to take dance lessons, a promise held out as consolation for moving again, but who is it who needs comfort? My mother plainly, emphatically, doesn't want to go, but the missile silos are done, the warheads lowered into place. There's no more work for my father in the desert, the landscape of my mother's heart. Work is at Cape Canaveral, where my father's going to build the structure in which the Apollo moon rocket will be assembled, the biggest building in the world (*You could fit seven football fields, or all of St. Peter's Cathedral . . .*).

I imagined Miss Tynes would be pleased when I told her about the dance lessons I'd been promised. But she said, "Oh, no, I hope it doesn't ruin you!" When I looked puzzled, she talked about spontaneity, unfettered movement, the limitations imposed by expectation and training—but still I don't think I understood. How could a teacher ever ruin how it felt to dance? Wasn't it always good to learn?

Our house in Florida is a motley pink stucco affair built around a little atrium, a square of open garden in whose sandy plot sprouts a rubber plant and mother-in-laws' tongues. Walls of glass surround the open space, so that from almost everywhere in the house you can see the damp sad things, which somehow manage to look more barren than tropical, a reminder of failure rather than evidence of fecundity.

Out back there's a big vacant lot that leads to the railroad tracks; there I catch an armadillo, which resembles a small pig wearing a suit of antique Japanese armor. I try to keep it in a cardboard box, and offer it lettuce and carrots, wilting items it adamantly refuses. That's the word for the armadillo: *adamant*, utterly defined by refusal. Its victory is all negation: the pasteboard liquor carton fills up with no, no, no. I let the beast go.

At twilight the town vehicle we call the mosquito truck rolls through the neighborhood, billowing a fog of DDT that thins out as it drifts across the yards. It's as if that fog clouds everything, the whole world heavy with moisture, subject to mildew. I think it is my mother's mood, ponderous, swelling, spilling out. I've seen a movie called *Donovan's Brain*, in which a man's brain, removed from his body and kept artificially alive, mushrooms and swells till it's monstrous, floating around the lab attached to an umbilical neural cord, threatening everybody. She attempts to continue painting, setting up her easel and little jars of turpentine in a corner of the living room, but her Florida landscapes are all stormy coasts, palm trees against a gray heaven's turbid atmosphere. The work stalls; she broods in the living room like Satan in Doré's illustrations for Dante's *Inferno*, up to his waist in the icy lake at the bottom of Hell. The easel abandoned, she fixes herself a vodka collins.

I am not off to a good start with my new fifth-grade teacher. In our first geography lesson, a review of the southern states, she uses her wooden pointer to identify the yellow shape of Texas on the unrolled wall map, and notes that one side of the state is bordered by the great river whose name she pronounces *RYE-oh Grand*.

I point out that since the name is Spanish, it is pronounced *REE-oh Grahn-day.*

She asks how I know and I point out that I read Spanish, and have seen the Rio in question, where it borders the city of Juarez, and that it is shallow, wide, and muddied with brick-red silt.

Well, she says, *this is America, and we say Rye-oh Grand.*

～

I go to Miss Stephanie's with my friend Jimmy Sunderland, the first person I have ever met who's as big a sissy as me. This is startling; he repels and entertains at once; he's funny, sometimes swooningly silly, with a butch waxed crew cut that seems too boyish for him. He is chubbier than me. (Our parents, in fact, have a hidden intent in paying for these after-school lessons; they want us to slim down.) Jimmy rhapsodizes about books or movies he loves in a way I find both familiar and embarrassing. I enjoy ferreting out the ways in which I feel superior to him, though I cannot express these since Miss Stephanie is his cousin, and the two of us comprise the entire boys' tap class. Secretly I feel he is not as smart as he pretends to be, and that his enthusiasm for show tunes somehow misses the point, as if he sees only their shiny surface, not their true grandeur.

I am studying two forms of dance. My parents have chosen ballroom dancing because my mother feels that the foxtrot, waltz, and cha-cha constitute useful elements of a young man's preparation for life. (What if, someday, you must admit that you don't know how to dance?) I study ballroom alone, so Miss Stephanie is my partner, though of course she is a great deal taller; my head comes just to her breasts. I am best at the cha-cha; I master the steps to the degree that Miss Stephanie (who is probably in her twenties and wears black leotards, her hair loosely piled on her head à la Lautrec) and I can actually become absorbed in the Latin flavor of the music. We cut an extravagant figure, once I get the hang of it, cha-chaing our way across the rectangular practice room, noticing ourselves in the mirrored wall.

On tap days Jimmy arrives to pick me up in his family car. We have already moved to another house, in a newer development atop what passes for a hill in Florida, a better address (Hillcrest

Drive, a street with a decidedly un-Floridian name), and the house comes with the strange accoutrement of a built-in bar. I get in the back seat with Jimmy while the silent driver, a black man in a dark jacket and cap, drives us to Miss Stephanie's; Jimmy makes no fuss about being chauffeured, so I don't either. The car's air-conditioned, the windows rolled up; we always drive with our windows open, trying, as my father says, "to beat the heat." To get to dancing school, the car must pass through what is called "the bad part of town," there is no way around it. As we do so the driver pushes a button that controls louvered blinds behind and beside us: we don't need to see.

But some vague image penetrates anyway, and lingers in memory: shantytown, gray wooden houses ramshackle on their bare lots, rusting tin roofs, roosters and chickens, old car seats and box springs, children with nothing to wear. The new money pouring in through NASA doesn't touch this neighborhood, and no one seems to consider that we're taking a limo through the ghetto in order for a white woman to teach us a fundamentally African American form of dance. Titusville, in 1963, is an apartheid state, though this is the year court-ordered integration comes to my school. One day a crowd of children and adults watch by the sidewalk at the far edge of the playground as a bus pulls up. Out come three small black girls. Nobody says a word, but the crowd parts, making a sort of aisle through which the heroines, in single file, march into their new world, defended by nothing but the notebooks and lunch boxes they carry before them like charms. Now we are integrated: in all my school's wash of white faces, three quiet African American children, who keep to themselves, armored in scrubbed cotton dresses. They are in a lower grade, so I never meet them. If they were in my class, would it be possible to meet them?

At Miss Stephanie's, Jimmy and I don our patent leather shoes with the metal cleats screwed to heel and toe. I think Jimmy looks a little ridiculous in his, especially when he wears short pants that highlight his chubby thighs. One day when he reveals that he doesn't know how to tie his shoes by himself, I mock him, then Miss Stephanie sets me straight: *Certainly there are some things that you don't know, Mark.* Obviously this is true, but what wounds is that I want to please Miss Stephanie, wish to court her favor, since she is my partner in the dizzy cha-cha, the tedious waltz.

For each tap lesson, Miss Stephanie plays records which feature a tinny piano and a nasal female voice which states commands: *shuf-FLE, ball change, shuf-FLE, ball change, re-PEAT*. The double long *e*'s of *repeat* pierce like little bee stings. We practice till we get it right, then we do it again.

∾

In 1997, en route to a Key West vacation, my boyfriend Paul and I decide to veer off the long, dull, forward pull of I-95 for a look at Titusville, which in my memory is all gray and gloom, a soulless strip spiteful even when it was new. I figure by now it's all Burger Kings and Winn-Dixies, but we might as well take a look. We drive off the exit ramp and—surprise!—Titusville's idiosyncratic and undeniably pretty: big white herons pose in the shallows, tropical trees shade the lazy gardens, downtown is decently preserved and full of character, and the old Florida woman in the doughnut shop, her skin waxed and mottled by fifty years of sunshine, couldn't be sweeter. There are a few little icons of the space years: murals of rockets, a high school team called the Astros, but it all seems to have settled into an unhurried calm, as if the dreamed-of boom never really happened and that's just fine. We even find Hillcrest Drive, which is well preserved and rather optimistic looking, the lawns decked with palms and crotons and small boats polished to a sun-catching sheen.

In sum, Titusville's attractive, balmy, and even marked by the sort of specificity of place which is getting rarer these days, which lets you know you couldn't be anywhere else.

So what was all the fuss about?

The horizon of childhood is a little one; the small field at the center of which a child stands seems almost infinitely rich, but it is still a small field. I couldn't see Titusville except through the dimming lens of my parents' points of view, and until I went back—sheer serendipity—I didn't understand just how shadowed their vision of the place had been. It makes me want to see the world, a little while, as they did, to understand what it was that loomed so large for them, that defined their Florida.

Every morning my father goes off to work in his sharply creased khaki pants. White government truck, white hard hat and chrome lunch box on the seat beside him, clipboard with schedules and figures involving the day's work. They're building on Merritt Island, a place that used to be a resort, but the government's taken the houses now, and they fade and crumble into the jungle like Mayan ruins. The island's a wild and snaky place; on the paved road through the swamps, you see rattlers hit by cars, stretched out on the asphalt, shorter than Arizona snakes, and big around in the middle, as if every one of them just swallowed a possum. Under one of the bulldozers at the site, my father said, a panther's made her den; the engineers have seen her with her cub. Where, when the bulldozer moves and they haul in the sleek components of the rocket, will she go?

He's gone early till suppertime, always meat and potatoes and a vegetable done to death, the Southern man's stock supper: pot roast, Swiss steak, pork chops, fried Spam with ketchup—just the menu for a chubby boy. Every day at four my mother says, *Well, I guess I should start supper*, halfhearted, going through the motions. Not much talk about his day, but there's some sense that the job's competitive, the work difficult, or the circumstances less than pleasant? Is he worried about money, since our move from the armadillo'd flats up to this fancier suburban place on a hill, where our retired neighbors even have a luminous blue swimming pool? When a hurricane comes, the benches from our picnic table float in the rippling aqua, along with a tree branch and a squadron of frogs.

Or is it my mother he's worried about, her moody and petulant reactions, her unshakable displeasure in this new world? Given all the moves, her history of adaptability, why is this time any harder? It used to be a simple thing, packing up the stuff of home, those familiar objects: the round, frameless mirror with the flamingos etched into the rim, the "rock maple" bureau with crocheted scarf, the chocolate-colored print, from my mother's childhood house, of two pointers in a field rigid with attention to something we won't ever see. Unpack the cartons, register at a new school, and there, we're home. But not anymore; it's as if she turned some corner, back in the desert, and ceased to be willing to start again.

I try to stand now in her place, looking toward her horizon, although my view is tentative, wavery. She's made it out of a relentless poverty; her mother, after all, lives in an unpainted, three-room shack that slopes like a funhouse at the fair. No paint or wallpaper inside, just bare boards to which my granny tacks collages she makes from pretty pictures cut from magazines. Outhouse down the hill, rows of sliced apples hung on string and drying from the roof, a big stick propped next to Granny's undulant featherbed in case snakes come in the house in the night. My mother's come from a place you don't get out of. And she'd been ill there, too, a year of rheumatic fever, so that when my father came to offer a bridge out of the old world she must still have been a little frail, and eager to step out of that circumscription.

Though it was also a place where she knew everybody, embraced by a family of seven kids; anywhere in that world she was somebody: Mary Stephens's girl, Mildred Stephens's sister. The first thing her handsome new husband had done was to move her straight to Puerto Rico, where he'd gotten a job building bridges on new roads in the mountains and the rain forest. Of course she hadn't known a soul, or a word of Spanish, and he was gone all day, sometimes nights, too, leaving her in the cool rooms they'd rented in a crumbling old house, grand once, with frangipani and monkeys in the garden, a drunken bank of gardenias dizzying beside the door. She'd befriended only her landlady, who'd send a servant to check under her beds for intruders in the evening, send mangoes on a tray. She was eighteen, alone most of the time, terrified, and yet in retrospect at least the stories of her two years on the island become her favorites, touchstones: *I used to ride the bus by myself, past rickety shacks built on stilts above the water, and I'd think, how do they ever stand up? I'd go to the market and oh, it was filthy, the meats hung on hooks and crawling with flies, but the fruit, and the flowers, I never saw such flowers.* . . . I think she's sorry, really, though exhilarated, when they have to get back to the mainland, because war's imminent; they take a steamer, the SS *Coamo*, from San Juan to New Orleans. I have a photograph of her on deck, a life preserver beside her ringed with the ship's name; she's in dark sunglasses and scarf, rather glamorous, inscrutable. Perhaps she's afraid. Nazi U-boats are rumored to be in the Gulf, and surely my father is going to war.

Here they are in another picture: he looking foolishly young in his white sailor suit and hat, she in a black-and-white polka-dotted dress and startlingly sexy black shoes. It's a shore leave; she's come to New Orleans to see him, and they're sitting on the concrete edge of an embankment of flowers and must have asked some stranger to take their picture.

Soon he is in the South Pacific, and she is pregnant with my sister, living with his parents on their chicken farm in East Tennessee—not especially prosperous, but something a bit better than subsistence: they have hens aplenty for my grandmother's velvet-and-air dumplings, and lard for her biscuits and cherry pies, whose rose-and-gold filling she canned herself, then baked till it bubbled up through the weightless lattice. My mother's there, I suppose, because they can feed her and her new baby, something her parents would probably find a strain if not an impossibility. Maybe her own parents' home is too much country, too much the rock-bottom rurality she's escaped; aren't they really, her people, hillbillies? But it isn't easy here; my grandmother's long-suffering, but she and her husband don't get along, and my grandfather's always trying to get my mother by herself, so that he can rub up against her or pat her ass. What is there to occupy her? It doesn't seem to occur to her or to anyone else—not now and not ever—that she might get a job, either for the war effort or, later, for company or stimulation or even money. She will never work, and on my grandparents' farm in 1944 she seems to be practicing for her isolation: writing letters to my father every day, letters he won't get for months, if ever. News leaking back, slowly, of the sinking of his ship; is he lost at sea? Intolerable waiting, then a telegram from him, and then he's sent out on another destroyer to do it all over again.

(Later he will hardly talk about it. A word or two about the ships going down, the raft, the days floating on the Pacific with few other men, no one and nothing else in sight. *No, I don't want to talk about it.*)

Maybe there's another reason she never works. When my sister went to Sweetwater by herself, in the sixties, to visit the relatives, my mother's sister and aunt said something like, "Well, how is

Ruth? She never was, you know, really right." I can't recapture the words, don't know what they said, exactly, but Sally understood them to mean that she was always fragile, unstable, not of the strong and reliable stock the farms of Sweetwater might be expected to produce.

Or is it that my parents have decided that she will devote herself to mothering, that she'll pour herself into the care and cultivation of us, who are her right and proper sphere? My sister's only two when the war ends; my parents begin their wanderings in the towns of Tennessee. Then there's that boy, stillborn, little occasion of grief buried in one of those places in the slipstream. When I learn as a child I would have had a brother, an older brother, even then I think how oddly different my life would have been, perhaps unrecognizable. My mother tells the story while she irons, lighting up another Salem. He has a little headstone somewhere, to this day I don't know where.

And then me, born when she's thirty-three and my father thirty-nine, delivered with a mass of fibroid tumors that also mean the end of her child-bearing. She'd expected a girl and named me Rachel Ann. *What do we call him?* Spur of the moment: Mark Alan, for no real reason.

Then years of moving, disconnections, though when we stay someplace a while she begins friendships, makes overtures: Daughters of the Eastern Star, PTA. Then we're gone again. But that's better, isn't it, than the alternative, back to those hardscrabble unpromising farms, back to houses with newspapers on the walls, the one warm room centered on the cookstove, an old iron pot of squirrel simmering with some long-canned okra, green beans slick with fatback?

Maybe that's what's depressing about Titusville, the soft-voweled tang of the South, too close to the bad old days. Though it's just like the way they talk about Puerto Rico: "That was a terrible life," they say. "Who'd want to go back there?" But in the stories life seems so vivid, so much more real than this one, some substance about it worth remembering.

Here in what my father called "Tight-Ass Ville" my parents don't make any friends, except for one couple, Al and Vi, who like to play cards. Card games are not high on my parents' list, but when they get together with Al and Vi, cards it is: pinochle, crazy eights. Al is wiry and easygoing, easy to like. He wears exotic short-sleeved shirts in tropical colors like lime and coral, which are never tucked in. Incipient emphysemic, he's permanently attached to a cigarette, but being quick to laugh, he frequently dissolves into fits of coughing that make conversation impossible. Vi is a blank to me: I find that my memory has completely replaced her with Vivian Vance: broad-hipped, salty and vivacious, quick with a retort. One evening they come to our house for cards; I am to make myself scarce somehow. I watch TV while they drink Tom Collinses and shuffle and deal under the orange plastic bubble of a lamp that hangs above our dining table. But something goes awry, something's said that shouldn't be, and the guests make an early departure. Then my mother and father let loose; I am uninvolved in their loud recriminations, but there's no getting away from their heated argument. I don't understand any of it, some dangerous and uninterpretable rage swirling around me I can't do anything to mend. They break a big kidney-shaped ashtray, its aqua glaze flecked with gold; they shatter a lamp. More dangerously, things seem broken on the inside, aswirl, destabilized. He sleeps on the couch in his underwear, she weeps in their bedroom, and in the morning some stunned version of it seems still to continue. I watch them like a wide-eyed spy, double-oh-seven, attempting to assess the damage. They move as if their heads and necks were fragile; they give each other a wide berth, and nobody talks to me. Eventually my father takes me to a movie, a matinee downtown, and when he brings me home she's still sitting at the dining table in her nightgown, looking out at the neighbor's pool through the sliding glass door and chain-smoking Salems. What does it matter what she wants? She's at the mercy of NASA, of the Army Corps of Engineers. She's survived backwoods poverty, illness, a world war, the death of a child, and twenty years of relative isolation, but will she survive Titusville?

∽

My mother tells of having the same dream, all her adult life: it's night in a strange city, she's walking, and suddenly she realizes she has no idea where in the world she is. No matter how long and how far she walks, there's nothing familiar, nothing to give her any clue; this street resembles a block in that city, but as soon as she thinks she knows where she might be something else contradicts it. How did she get here, and where is the here she's gotten to? The doors don't open, the streets don't turn onto any known corner, any landmark of home. And when she wakes she's just as panicked, just as lost, till she remembers where she is.

∿

There's a song I like on the radio, "Sukiyaki," a sentimental ballad sung in Japanese by a male singer, and one day I'm listening to a program where listeners are invited to call in and request a song; the asked-for tune will be played with a dedication, first names only, such as "This is going out from Johnny to Sylvia. . . ." I think of a boy I like at school, a shorter boy with wavy blond hair and a winning giggle, so I call up the radio station. Soon I'm in the car with my parents headed for the shopping center, and suddenly there it is, "going out from Mark to Stevie. . . ." I grin in the backseat, amazed, then I blush. Suddenly it feels too hot, claustrophobic in the car. I've written something on the air, all by myself, and it hangs there, almost visible, as if I can see the aftereffect of sound. I focus my attention on the green vinyl of the backseat, the strips of woven upholstery that run up and down. Did I want my parents to hear what I'd done?

∿

That fall we see Martin Luther King on television and my father calls him Martin Luther Coon. My mother says, "Hush, Larry." I befriend two small girls who have moved into a house across the street, children of black parents who work for NASA. The neighborhood ripples, albeit quietly. Yolanda and Yohanna's mother invites me to baby-sit, since I am such a nice boy, and when the parents go out on the town (hard to feature, in Titusville), I do my supervisory work with pride: we color, watch TV, have a snack, and the girls are in bed almost on time. I've never been in a black family's house before; it's odd that everything's just like our house, only nicer, fresher, as if the operations of the household, its daily maintenance, were conducted with a different kind of optimism, with faith.

I'm in school when the president is shot, in science class, and the whole school files into the cafeteria to sit at the long pinkish Formica dining tables and watch the continuous broadcast from Dallas. What does it mean? Here memory adds a detail that defies chronology: while we watch the broadcast from Dealey Plaza, I'm sitting next to a girl named Paula, who has had her dark hair cut in a new way, a Beatle cut, and she actually does look like Paul McCartney, as evidenced by the hundreds of Beatle cards she brings to school in an upholstered case. Some girls, while we watch Walter Cronkite in his skinny tie and glasses, are weeping, and some are quietly passing, beneath the table, Paula's Beatle cards.

In our depression, my mother and I have both turned to food for solace, and she soon determines that the exercise I'm getting in dance class is not enough; some additional measure must be taken to deal with the issue of our hips. We visit a doctor and each receive a prescription for diet pills, the popular new amphetamines.

These, indeed, lend to daily life a certain fizz and glitter. I dance with more spark and vigor, and my mother develops an interest in fishing. Some days (am I home from school? is it some holiday or weekend when my father's working?) she and I go out to remote places, some quiet pier along the Indian or Banana River; we catch yellowtail, brilliant flatfish as fresh and sunny looking as sliced lemons. Over cups of black coffee (yellow plastic cups, a new kind of "china" called Melmac, curvaceous and unbreakable) and lots of cigarettes, she sits at the kitchen table and talks about kinds of fish, colors and textures of scales, new places we might try out. On one of our outings we discover the Dummit Plantation, a ruined old cypress house, boarded up, in the dark heart of an ancient orange grove, shaggy palm trees bending in the rain, bright birds flitting and calling as if they owned the place, evidence of an old Florida far from the flattened world of our cul-de-sac, our shopping center with its grocery and its Woolworth's lined up beside the paved lake of parking lot.

I have a new pastime, after school, which involves the shopping center. I like to walk there, through the sandy pine grove where our development stops, and across the busy street to the Woolworth's, which has not only a soda fountain but a number of booths upholstered in tufted red vinyl. I like to sit in one of these booths and order a Cherry Coke, and then sip it slowly and wait to see if I can meet someone to talk to. In my mind I call this game "picking someone up." (Have I learned this phrase at the movies? Have I already seen, on late afternoon TV, Geraldine Page in *Summer and Smoke*, the delicate Southern spinster Miss Alma, after her ruination by unrequited love, headed out to the soda fountain where she can pick up a traveling salesman?) I talk to boys, older ones, since there aren't too many fifth-graders hanging out at the dime store looking to make friends. If I focus on making this happen, I can get a boy to talk to me; then I can make myself funny and interesting, I discover, and he'll like me and keep talking to me. The pills help; I seem to possess a new reserve of conversational sparkle. I ask questions, flatter the boys with my interest, my insight and ease. I understand, as if intuitively, that I'm not going to see them again. They're not really going to be my friends. I just like to find out that they could be, a while, that I can make myself lively enough that an older boy, maybe even a boy in high school, will sit and have a Coke with me. I like having that kind of power.

I associate our fishing trips with sunlight and the bright fauvist color of the yellowtails, but one trip turns dark. It's a weekend, and my father's taken us out on Merritt Island, to a place we couldn't go except that he works for the government. It's an old pier that sticks out into the water, some of its planks missing so you have to be careful; the land all around it is jungle, just a little mosquitoey path winding to the pier, which is sturdy even though abandoned. Nothing's biting, but we persist, still there at twilight, and then something fierce takes hold of my father's line, which goes waggling and zigzagging all over the place till he exhausts the creature and pulls it in: a black, slick yard of pure muscle, a three-foot eel writhing and rippling on the oily planks of the pier. My mother screams, my father shouts and grabs his machete, and with a quick chop he slices it right in half, but the eel doesn't stop moving. And he doesn't stop his chopping; he brings the blade down over and over again, keeps hacking till the thing's only a scattered mess of the smallest scraps, black little pieces of meat, as if it were the most revolting thing in the world and no one could rest until it bore no resemblance to itself.

Then nobody says a word about it. We pack up our tackle boxes and sit in the front seat of the government truck for the long drive home, and nobody says a word.

∾

I am tap-dancing with a vengeance, and slimming down, so that the trousers of my costume for the dance recital must be taken in already, though they were ordered only a couple of weeks ago. My part of the recital is a performance as Uncle Sam, dressed in flag-striped satin pants and vest and a particularly fabulous blue-sequinned drum-major hat, with a white furry brim and a resplendent, spiky plume of metal foil coming right out of the crown, towering above my forehead. I am the centerpiece of a performance of "Seventy-six Trombones," and I do my tap routine surrounded by five little girls in sequined outfits like bathing suits dipped in glitter. They march and twirl batons (I am fascinated by batons, but do not have one) around me in shifting patterns. We don't have to worry about a part for Jimmy Sunderland, who has dropped out of tap school. Perhaps he can't keep up with my new, chemically enhanced enthusiasm?

As the recital approaches, I keep my costume in a box in my dresser drawer and take it out for frequent examination. The marvelous hat gleams on the dresser, poised all night before its double in the mirror. I dance in the costume just once before the performance, for a dress rehearsal, which goes without a hitch. And that evening is, indeed, flawless: the adoring audience of parents cheers, right in the middle of the dance, while I am doing a series of time steps, my arms circling around and around me in the air, my attendant sylphs twirling their brains out. The applause intoxicates me. My dance feels timeless to me, as if I'm weightless, an astronaut in a space capsule; I can float in the air over the darkened recital hall, over the spotlight in which my body executes, without a hitch, the timed and clattering steps of the dance. This is what becomes of the firebird, drugged and trained: everyone adores him.

∾

My father likes *The Lawrence Welk Show*, an awful bore of bland music and constant smiling, and *The Ed Sullivan Show*, which is more interesting, since it offers bits and pieces of disparate worlds: some circus, some Hollywood, a little Broadway. One evening Agnes Moorehead is featured, reciting a passage from Proust.

She wears a long chiffon evening gown with many filmy layers which wrap her throat and arms; they're bluish gray, like everything on our TV screen, but you can tell from the context that the studio audience can see that Miss Moorehead is swathed in mauve, since the passage she is reading is in fact a celebration of mauve. The speaker is walking down a street when he spies Madame Swann, in her carriage, and what transports him is her complete enwrapment in that color; she has become a sort of ambassador for mauve, mauve's priestess and celebrant. It's as if the color itself has gone out riding in a carriage, to take the air, to give the admiring world the rapture and benefit of its charms.

Miss Moorehead is transfixed by her text; she is all enunciation, long vowels, consonants emphasized by the sure, firm movements of tongue and teeth, arms lifted and turned so that her own mauve veils move in a breeze of her own making.

Then comes Topo Gigio the talking mouse, or a man who spins dozens of plates on sticks at once, but who cares? A new seed's planted in my head, a new constellation of elements: chiffon, elocution, "mauve" (wonderfully unnecessary word, putting on airs, making "lavender" seem ordinary). Something to be savored, unwrapped: *Proust*.

My latest enchantment lies in the realm of the theater, in performance. On a trip to Sarasota, we encounter a bracing splash of Europe: John Ringling's marble tomb of a museum full of darkly varnished old masters, more Circumcisions and Salomes than you could, as my father says, "shake a stick at." Ringling's villa on the tropic waterside has emerald cut-glass chandeliers. I like best the theater he bought in Italy, in the town of Asolo, and brought to Florida in numbered pieces, packed in crates. Reassembled, it's a Renaissance music box, a horseshoe of gilt and velvet tiers, a blue ceiling studded with golden stars. We see *Twelfth Night* there, and laugh at the Clown's reading a letter to Viola in a wild, distorted voice. Told to speak normally, he explains, "I do but read madness," and my whole family laughs. I don't understand the implications of the play's playfully twisted genders, the comedy of cross-dressing, though I don't imagine these are entirely lost on me either; I put them away for later, like Proust. What I'm aware of loving is light and costume, the shifting charm of theatrical effect.

Back home I construct a paper proscenium and stage, and begin to make my own designs: watercolored paper cut-outs for trees and pavilions, figures from magazines to represent Clown and Duke, Olivia and Viola. I'm planning to make a sort of puppet version of the play, all in my own design, but I get only as far as the opening. My cardboard Clown, in harlequin diamonds, strums a cardboard lute: "If music be the food of love, play on. . . ."

Is it love that music feeds? On a trip to Orlando (no megaresort in those days, but a bigger town, with a shopping center, an escape from the confines of Titusville), I am set loose on my own in Jordan Marsh while my parents wander separately somewhere in the big department store. I have a small stash of dollars. I gravitate toward the records, I stroll the bins until I come to the section labeled opera, as if its pull were gravitational. I flip through the single and boxed albums with their lovely, fragrant names: *Tannhäuser, La Forza del Destino, La Traviata*: all mysteries, no evidence as to what they contain but the titles and the cover photographs: women with imposing domes of hair, brushed up from the forehead, their makeup heavy, their shaped eyebrows and muscled throats also imposing. How do you ever choose one, where do you begin? I linger a long time, and at last, because I have no criteria by which to make a decision, I choose something hastily, almost arbitrarily, because it has a friendly-looking pink cover and appears to be a comedy, a man and woman in Versailles satins and powdered wigs making faces at each other across the pink field. I carry my purchase to the counter, count out the bills, meet my parents with my first opera album, the first record I have ever bought for myself, in a plain brown bag. I display it: *Don Pasquale*, by Donizetti. "Oh," they say. "Oh." At home, played on the big cabinet stereo whose wooden lid lifts to reveal turntable and controls, the record proves difficult to listen to; it is, after all, in Italian, and seems to spin around some axis I can't apprehend, as if it involved not just one language I don't know but several.

The kids in my neighborhood put on a play, *Tom Thumb's Wedding*. What Tom Thumb has to do with it I never discern, since what the play actually consists of is a mock marriage ceremony, organized by Pam, who lives across the street. Pam is a chunky, breezy blond who gets things done; she organizes a surprisingly large number of children to take part in the pageant, which will take place in her garage. I am pleased that she has invited me to perform the role of the Preacher, who is the only person in the piece with anything to say; I read the ceremonial lines pasted into a Bible while everyone else has merely to march in and look solemn. Pam herself takes the role of the Bride, of course, and strides in, pink cheeked and *zaftig* in her white dress, while very tiny children walk in front of her scattering petals. Every kid for blocks is part of the array, except Yolanda and Yohanna—not invited, or have they, by now, moved away? Everyone comes and goes, children of space. Although there is only one rehearsal, the performance is a huge success, attended by enthusiastic parents, and I am so inspired that I conceive a plan for a show of my own.

My friend Werner will assist. He is a sweet and unassuming boy whom I like because he's nice and because he will do anything I say. He has curly dark hair and beautiful olive skin; his father is a German scientist, his mother from Mexico. His skin color must make him a bit of an outsider in Titusville, and maybe that's another reason we're friends. For months we've been exploring and colonizing an island we've discovered, in a raw place where the palmetto scrub's been bulldozed for a new subdivision. The raw, mounded earth is pinkish-orange, with big exposed chunks of a soft compacted stuff called coquina, a sort of layer cake of old shells. The builders have gouged out a hole which is filled with water of a particularly toxic-looking shade, a poisonous mixture of aqua and pistachio; in the center of this diminutive lagoon is an island. I say, "Werner, let's build a bridge," and he says, "Okay." Then I say, "Werner, this island is a new continent," and he says, "Yeah."

So Werner is quite amenable to participation in my performance. He is to play the bongos, which he seems to enjoy, sitting on the floor with the drums between his knees, head down, beatnik-style, immersed in slapping out rhythms. We practice with some records, but for the heart of the show I will sing a cappella while I dance in the appropriate costume. We play with different numbers, consider the possibilities, and while I don't recall the potential songs we discarded, I can't forget the song I chose as my vehicle, the number I could completely throw myself into, which was a version of Judy Garland singing "Get Happy."

I must have seen this on Garland's TV show, which, even at ten, I understood to be an amalgam of glamour and damage so peculiar as to both transfix and unsettle at once. I don't think we own the record—my parents don't care for her, not really—but somehow it seems that every word of the tune is already imprinted on my memory, as if I were born knowing it: "*Shout hallelujah, come on get happy,/Get ready for the judgment day.*" Somewhere I've found a red chiffon scarf, just the thing to hold for the performance, and a shiny black cane. I'm planning to locate black stockings and a tux jacket so I can achieve the whole look.

Cut to: film version. The room is dramatically dark, only a small spotlight on Werner as he begins the bongo roll, which crescendos and bursts emphatically, then a two-beat pause and out from behind our makeshift curtain I pop, all legs and angles, strutting sideways, my voice low and quiet, syncopating the song's opening bars. Then, at a subtle signal from me, the bongos go nuts, and all the contained energy I've barely been suppressing breaks loose, my voice rising on the stressed syllables:

We're GO-ing cross the RI-ver
for to get to the other side,
We're GO-ing cross the RI-ver
Milk and honey on the other side.

Now I'm in my full stride, my smile wide and glittering in the spot, my fingers spread wide in the air minstrel-style, then flying up to lift my top hat in rhythm. I am amphetamine bright and glittering on the inside, too, possessed by my song. I am entirely a Judy, right down to the prescriptions, in tight black stockings, the tuxedo jacket slicing across her thighs just below the waist, eyes huge with the force pouring out of her gaze now into the music. I begin to wave the long red scarf in the air, making it also dance to my song and the throb of my accompaniment. I toss my cane away and hold the scarf high over my head with both hands. I hold it behind my back and my behind, pull it back and forth in a kind of shimmy.

Knock at my bedroom door, loud, uncompromising, not to be ignored. The music in my head diminishes and twists away, the real bongos sputter and cease, lights up, movie's done. It's my mother at the door.

What would you say if you found your ten-year-old son performing a drag show?

My mother says, *Son.*

I haven't learned to recognize it yet, the look on her face, the crinkled skin around the eyes, the mouth somehow fallen, but I recognize it now, in memory: she's drunk.

She says, *Werner, you get on home now.*

She says, *What are you doing?*

I say, *Werner and I are putting on a show*, explaining about *Tom Thumb's Wedding*, and how there will be many musical numbers, how we're going to sell tickets, and even as I'm saying it I know I wasn't really planning to do these things. Only a game. No, more than that: what I liked was the daydream of the performance, how I could feel utterly free, dreamed and improvised Judy, because Werner wasn't about to judge anything.

She says, "You can't do that for the neighbors."

Now I'm wilting; whatever flamed up in me in my singing is wavering and chilly now. I know, all the way through, that she isn't going to love me the same way now. Am I standing there with the filmy piece of red chiffon limp in my hand? Am I wearing her lipstick? I feel blank; I have no explanations.

She says, with a hiss, with shame and with exasperation, *Son, you're a boy.*

And now a performance begins again, this time not a movie but a play, no set for this one but darkness, one little island of light in which a boy and his mother stand, in absolute silence, as if there were a vacuum around them, and the play has begun just as their dialogue is over. Nothing else to say. It's a stopping place. How can they move? They're held there in the mother's disappointment, her fear for what her son will become. His dissolute future spreads out in front of her like an oil slick: shameful, worthless, sick.

And they're held frozen also in the son's fear and shame, since of course he *knows* he's a boy, doesn't need reminding. The fact that she feels she must tell him this means he has failed: he isn't who she wanted, he absolutely does not know how to be who she wanted. And wasn't he also somehow like her, wasn't he coming close to who she was, herself a vulnerable Judy, jazzed on a vodka-and-speed cocktail of her own devising?

"You're a boy" means, *I'm policing you now, we've got your number, we see your deviant ways. You must be vigilant, impossibly vigilant, because you could slip anytime, you could make so many mistakes, you don't even know what the mistakes are, since you don't understand what it is you're supposed to be.*

You can't hide from us now.

No—it means, *Hide, hide as far as you can; what we already know we will put away from us, in a rigid little case, we will tuck it away in a hole, like bread buried in a jar in the garden.* Echo of Khrushchev on a TV screen, pounding and shouting: "We will bury you."

Or worse, *We will teach you to bury yourself for us.*

You're a boy: watershed between childhood and something else. I have been ushered into the world where adults live; I have been warned, have been instructed to conceal my longing. And though I will understand, someday, that without longing there'd be nothing to carry us forward, that without longing we wouldn't be anyone at all, I can't see that now. I'm a child, or I was until she said, *You're a boy*. I am stunned and silent, caught in a shame that seems to have no place to come to rest. I have been initiated—whether because my mother wanted to punish or to protect me—into an adult world of limit and sorrow.

PART TWO

7

Guest from Nowhere

Transfer. I sleepwalk through sixth grade, our year in Northern California, gray plain of the valley above Sacramento, acre on acre of almond trees, bare all the rainy gray winter. Somnambulist, I cannot be reached.

I'm a chubby smart bookish sissy with glasses and a Southern accent, newly arrived from unimaginable places. It's obvious that even the teacher, an ex-military brute with a blond brush cut and missing fingers lost to a bomb in Korea, thinks I'm weird. I walk the outer edge of the playground at recess. I like to walk with my arms bumping against my hips in a repetitive rhythm, an enjoyable beat; I can lose myself in a little song of my own making and not think. The other kids—who've grown up in Maryville and have known each other forever—are glad to have some stranger do something strange to identify himself and solidify their bond. They notice, and howl, and I vow never to do this absent-minded thing again. But walking alone another day, unsure what else to do with myself, I forget, and they cry out with delight.

Then and there I began to be sure that my feelings weren't like anyone else's: I existed in a special zone, no one felt what I did. Held at a distance from others: that was both the price and the reward. And it seemed unbridgeable, the gap between that private richness inside and the hopeless, hapless way I was seen. "Between us and you," the Bible says, "there is a great gulf fixed." To this day I catch myself feeling startled sometimes when someone expresses a feeling or impression just like mine; I expect to be the only one of my kind, alien passing through, guest from nowhere.

For Christmas I wanted a basketball. This was an accommodation on my part; I didn't really care for sports, but basketball didn't seem overwhelmingly physical, and it was something you could play by yourself, and I was tall, and maybe. . . . There were other boys who'd walk to the playground after school, alone, and shoot baskets. When I unwrapped the gift, it *was* what I'd asked for, but my parents had chosen a basketball of a special sort, a marbleized sphere swirled in green and purple. It was pretty, in truth, but my heart sagged; I'd envisioned a real boy's ball, plain orange, defined by mysterious black lines, and the soap-bubble swirl of my new ball reinforced what I already knew, really, that the regulation equipment of the game wasn't to be my lot.

Well, all right then—if I can't fit, I'll be an ozone boy, more rarefied, more peculiar. I'll breathe the atmosphere of my own elevation; I will be doggedly devoted to my own peculiarity. I'll show you how to be alone!

That's the queer boy's dynamic, simultaneously debased and elevated. Even if no one but you—*especially* when no one but you—is witness to your triumph, still, you can embrace your own difference. Inside the rejected boy, inside the unloved body, reigns the sissy triumphant, enraged, jeweled by an elegant crown of his own devising.

∾

For a very long time I believed we were powerless in the grip of the Army Corps of Engineers, that transfers were just an inevitable consequence of the kind of work my father did; it wasn't till years after

my mother died that he started talking one day about all the bas-
tards he'd worked for, how he had a knack for saying the thing that
nobody wanted to hear, and so it was hard to get along with super-
visors: sometimes he'd just quit before they fired him, or some-
times they'd take the initiative and tell him to move on. This came
as a bit of a revelation; all this time I'd thought of our moves as pas-
sive, visited upon us, and suddenly it seems we couldn't stay in one
place because my father couldn't get along with people. Another
move: unpacking the boxes, arranging the paintings she'd brought
along, my mother must have wondered how long we'd stay this
time, must have wondered if any plan she'd make might last.

Why didn't I see this before? He clearly couldn't get along with
us; his taciturn surface would erupt, now and then, into something
abrasive and unfeeling. "Us"—are she and I a unit, joined by our
common opposition to him? That's how I think of it, sometimes,
my mother and I joined by our sensitivity, our common tastes. I'm
her ally, bound to her by character and personality, though I don't
always think I'm the ally she wants.

At my school there's a little model of the solar system, a ma-
chine my teacher called a Tripanzee planetarium. Turn the crank
and colored glass balls move around in orbits, mimicking the pat-
tern of planets in their rings around the fixed yellow globe of the
sun. Some planets have moons affixed, smaller spheres that circle
the larger bodies they're bound to. My father and I spin around my
mother like that, as if we're both bound to her larger gravitation; is
that why I can't see him, quite, because the larger pull of her ob-
scures him?

∾

Transfer: Lancaster, California, in the Antelope Valley, the desert
above LA—the childhood home of Judy Garland, though I didn't
know that then. Spiky, lunar-looking Joshua trees ringed our
neighborhood drive-in theater, at the edge of the suburb, where I'd
go and watch awful movies from an air-conditioned bank of seats
upstairs over the concession stand: Olivia de Havilland in *Lady in a
Cage*, Vincent Price and Annette Funicello in *Dr. Goldfoot and the
Bikini Machine*.

Here I devote myself to the pursuit of a sort of aggressive nor-
mality—the result of that awful, lonely sixth-grade year, and my

mother's warning, my own sense of difference, and the advent of junior high, with its overwhelmingly social culture, its new emphasis on submerging individual life in the culture of the group. I don't know how to be a normal kid, and since I am attempting to accomplish something I have absolutely no idea how to do, the result is simply nervousness, a constant sense of tension. I cannot relax into the sort of unself-consciousness that conveys normality: I must monitor my gestures, my appearance, my voice. And so I have achieved a sort of identity as a smart, nerdy boy, my movements as stiff as my hair, which I lacquer into place each day before school with my mother's Aqua Net.

I obviously cannot be a Jock like Roger Woods and his blond friend Mike, who make fun of me on the bus ride home; I don't know the rules, am uncoordinated, and have in essence detached my head from my body, that unreliable source of grief and trouble. I cannot be a Regular Guy like Ed Fernandez, who is distinguished by being a boy everyone likes, the result of his easy attitude of acceptance. (One day in PE we're playing flag football, which I loathe; the rules are mysterious, and involve wearing a little strip of cloth attached to your shorts, which others try to pull off. We divide into two teams, Shirts and Skins; I am horrified that I am a skin, and I refuse to strip; I will not be seen by these boys. Ed Fernandez, who's also pudgy, and also sprouting hair like me, is the only boy who doesn't mock me. He says, "Hey, I'm fat too, it's okay," but I am too stiff and afraid to be grateful for his sanity.)

Of the available categories I choose Brain. I favor cardigan sweaters in argyle, and plaid shirts buttoned all the way to the collar, and am twice voted Most Likely to Succeed. My social studies report, an account of an imaginary journey to Europe, becomes a huge, overblown affair, involving hundreds of pictures cut from old *National Geographic*s, and a narrative of almost obsessive tediousness describing the sights I've seen, its text like a fantastic, repetitive, and pointless novel written by a lunatic. I've typed it carefully, using the skills I've learned from a book I bought, *Touch Typing in Ten Easy Lessons*.

These rather clueless attempts to be a good boy do not preclude a certain flirtation with cool. Where does it come from, this sudden attraction to style, an intimation—covert at first, carefully hidden—that the stylish might have something to do with me, might be something I could partake of? My school bus ride is tolerable only because the loudspeakers on the school bus play a good radio station, and I can tune out the evil Roger and Mike with the music of the Rolling Stones; I can't stop singing "Ruby Tuesday," from *Between the Buttons*, an album on whose cover the band's faces melt in stylish distortion. I—like? am attracted to?—a boy named Tom Hutch, a smart and likable kid with a beefy body and blond hair crew-cut and waxed into angularity; Tom's older brother lives in Los Angeles, and he sends back items which have about them the unmistakable flavor of the new: a photographic self-portrait in a polka-dot shirt with a long, pointy collar, looking thoughtful in a bathroom mirror. He lives in an apartment in the city, Tom says, alone. Strange possibility, I think, unimaginable. He sends a poster from a concert, its unfamiliar lettering oddly organic, as if it's in motion. He sends an album of peculiar music by Frank Zappa and the Mothers of Invention, and Tom and I pay close attention to its distortions and funny lyrics: *Suzy Creamcheese, what's got into you?* We know we're supposed to like it, and we do.

Tom and I go to a concert at Antelope Valley Community College. I've never been to a rock concert before, and I don't know what to expect; I go because there's a pop song on the radio I like called "Yellow Balloon," and the band who sings it is opening the concert, warming up for the main act, a band I've never heard of called the Byrds. When my father drops us off, everyone's very excited about the Byrds, and soon we're part of a crush of people in the lobby of the concert hall, which the Byrds, who are late, must pass through when they arrive. Mounting heat, then a wave of apprehension: here they are, pale and long-haired, in lush tapestry shirts and leather hats. I've never seen people like them; they have an aura of otherness about them, the future's unfamiliar ozone. My Yellow Balloon–men seem flimsy beside them, cheerful little bits of fluff; the Byrds play with a sort of urgent whiny insistence, the light show (another thing I've never seen before) throbbing and pulsing behind them, a dilating wheel of colored light filled with kaleidoscopic pulses: jellyfish, mandalas, explosions of stars. They sing "Mr. Tambourine Man" and "Eight Miles High"; they sing like they mean it.

Home, I appropriate our slide projector. We've abandoned the slide shows of masterpieces anyway, and I experiment with methods of creating light shows of my own. How can I get those pulsing organic shapes? Watercolors, crayons, Jell-O, and Saran Wrap? I make stabs at synchronization with my new records (the Mamas and the Papas, the Association)—and considerable messes.

Tom sleeps over at my house one night, and when it's time for bed he strips to his underpants, which look especially white beside his tanned belly. He sleeps with the sheet pulled across his midriff, so that his nipples are exposed. When my eyes are accustomed to the darkness, when I think he's sleeping, I watch him. But then I see his eyes open a little, he knows I'm watching, so I quickly force myself to close my eyes. Soon our friendship cools.

On a trip to Los Angeles, given some money and time on my own at the Topanga Canyon Mall, I return to rendezvous with my parents with purchases which startle even myself: a pair of brown plaid pants with flared bottoms, a cream-colored turtleneck, and a thick brown belt of notable width. The remarkable thing is that I have not only purchased these items for myself, but am *wearing* them. I've even combed my hair down from the imprisonment of its rigid wave into bangs. One moment I'm my regular, buttoned-up self, and then I emerge from the dressing room in the department store and say, "I'll take these; I'm going to wear them." Suddenly I'm aware that no one around me knows what I used to look like; they can only see me as I am now, this kid in his new outfit, with an obvious flair for style. So that I must entirely startle my parents, appearing as I do beside the shopping mall's tropic waterfall at the appointed time, incarnation of the new.

∽

I love Petula Clark singing "Downtown." Pet, they call her on the radio, but I prefer Petula, with its aura of another country, another life. She sounds both young and wise at once, but when she appears on *The Ed Sullivan Show*—in a short black dress with a lace collar, standing perfectly still but sometimes swinging her arms from side to side in a carefully planned movement, tilting her head just so at the right passage in the lyric—you can see she's been around enough to earn the right to give advice.

The tune is cheerful, but marked by the recognition of struggle, as the very first words explain:

When you're alone and life is making you lonely
You can always go—Downtown.
When you've got worries all the noise and the hurry
Seems to help I know—Downtown.

In only four lines she's made it clear that she understands exactly how it feels to be alone and worried; thus she is every teenage kid's coconspirator. *I know*, she says; she understands me at a distance, which is exactly how I long to be understood. Petula understands that anonymous comfort which is one of adolescence's great and only consolations: hanging out, wandering around, getting lost in the world that's larger than your family. Especially when you come from a little nuclear knot of trouble, it's hard to feel the space around yourself in which you can come to be unknown. And you can't go on being known in the old ways; you need to disappear a little in order to come back as someone new: yourself. You have to go—Downtown.

To do so is to do nothing, admittedly, about the circumstances that made you lonely and worried in the first place. But that's exactly the point: you can't do anything about those things now. Petula says, *Listen, you can't fix anything yet, you aren't ready, your sadness and isolation cannot be solved, but here's something you can have which is full of promise, full of what's to come next.* Thus she has proclaimed herself as every gay boy's friend; she sees us in our isolation and extends her song to us, proving her friendship by being the first to suggest that there's actually something we can *do* about our situation: get up and get yourself downtown.

You can take a form of power over what you essentially cannot change, because you step out of it all, a little bit, become less yourself while the colored lights shine on the wet streets. These are the wisest words ever spoken to gay children: "You can always go—Downtown." Maybe, she sings, you'll even find someone there "who's just like you." Later, yes—not just yet. The important thing, Petula instructs us, is to join something larger than ourselves, a stream of lights and lives: movie shows, the bossa nova, and my favorite suggestion:

Maybe you know little places to go to
Where they never close—Downtown.

I don't, of course. In Lancaster there is no such place, just the silvery screen of the drive-in, lonely in the moonlight, surrounded by the stark silhouettes of the Joshua trees. But Petula says it's out there someplace, count on that.

And if I can't go there, at least I can buy some stylish clothes at the mall, and begin to get ready.

$\sim$

My parents don't have much energy to notice, dealing as they are with their own confrontation with the new. "Your father," my mother tells me, "has cancer, and we don't know how long he's going to live"; the statement's that plain and straightforward. The cancer is a melanoma, a blue-black mole on his back the color of my childhood experiments with mold on bread. It had been there always but suddenly bloomed. By the time his doctor sent him to a surgeon at UCLA, who'd cut the silver-dollar-size invader from the center of his back, it was too late; the cancer had gone into his lymph nodes, and from there it seemed only a matter of time, and perhaps not much at that.

We drive to UCLA once a week, where I walk around Westwood (bracing sense of a city, magazine stores, cafés, unknown life) while he goes to chemotherapy, some experimental procedure involving large doses of estrogen. The side effects are unpleasant: paler, weak some days, plagued by diarrhea, losing body hair, and developing breasts, he keeps working anyway.

A new sort of campaign begins, to ensure that my father and I have time together while we can; it isn't spoken, exactly, but I understand that the intention is that I will remember him in these ways. He takes me places: to a Chinese temple, with a flowery Confucian altar crowded with gods, where men toss yarrow sticks and the air's sweet with thick incense. On a hike into the Sierras, a long hike to a place called Feather Canyon Falls; it must be awful for him, really, walking the nine miles in and out with me, weak as he feels, but we want to reach the falls, which seems the point of the hike through the dark shade of the evergreens. He wants me to have this adventure with him.

But it's a doomed campaign, in essence, since there isn't a connection between us already; we don't feel that click which can't quite be willed, and there's never a sense of real ease between us.

I wonder if—when he bent his face to kiss the top of my infant head—something about me smelled different, some whiff on the skin signaling: *You will never be entirely at home with this boy*? Or did it take a while, until the first gesture or phrase or tilt of the hips that made him stop and assess me, apprehending—did he name it to himself, directly?—what he hadn't seen before.

Or did I choose the distance myself? It's not as if my father hasn't made a habit of gestures of affection: my whole life, ungrudging, he's driven me to the movies, paid for my ticket and my candy and my phone call for a ride home. I have a vague memory of banana splits at a drugstore soda fountain back in Tennessee, every Sunday after church. I remember him taking me to a drive-in, back in Tucson, the year of Mikey's death, when some deeply stupid movie I wanted to see was playing only there, and in my second-grade rapture with the work of Edgar A. Poe I simply *had* to see it; he'd endured the whole thing, bought popcorn, and we'd watched Vincent Price melt right on screen, after his rotting body had been abandoned by whatever awful immaterial force had animated him. And over the years he'd always slip me cash, the bills increasing—ones to fives, tens to twenties—as our family fell apart.

I do not think he wanted to be far away from me, but somehow he's resolutely unavailable, the life of feeling sealed away in him, nearly impossible to reach. He doesn't say what he feels or thinks for a long time, so that such statements emerge finally under pressure, awkward, hot, unkind. Slow to speak, because it was dangerous for him to feel? At twelve, of course, I don't see any of that. The hike is something for me to get through, though I like dark woods, the plummet and spume of the falls, which do feather out in the air, and I know I'm supposed to keep this walk in my memory: an Experience with my Father.

∾

I have a new PE teacher, Mr. Kablutis, who is ugly but undeniably fascinating. He's a tall, angular, awkward guy whose parts don't seem quite matched, and everything about him is knobby or hairy:

big knees and elbows, big calf muscles and shoulders, crew cut over a big nose which holds up his big plastic glasses. We make fun of his name, which seems as awkward as he does. We don't have a locker room in the eighth grade, but a classroom whose windows are covered over with black construction paper because the boys are required to change, for PE, into red cotton shorts, T-shirts, sneakers, and—the essential thing—jockstraps. What are they for, these odd elastic contraptions that lift our twelve-year-old genitals and frame our buttocks with their wide straps? We sit at desks to change, and put our clothes on the wire shelf underneath us. I hate this; I don't want anyone to see my unclothed body. I know there's something wrong with it, especially when I start to sprout dark pubic hair, something that seems out of place, mistaken, impossible. I become obsessed with the idea that I don't want anyone to see my new pubic hair; somehow it's the absolute locus of shame. I borrow a razor from my parents' bathroom cabinet and shave it off, but then I look doubly ridiculous, pink and scraped, the stubble sprouting again, and I wriggle around in my desk chair, trying to hide myself beneath the square foot of Formica desktop.

Since there's no office or cubicle, some days Mr. Kablutis changes too, at the teacher's desk in front of us. A strange transformation, one I take in deeply, though I know I'm not to look at him steadily but must steal glances while I appear to be busying myself with my tube socks or my shoelaces. Off come his nerdy glasses with the hunk of tape holding the frames together at the temple; off comes the ugly shirt, the chiseled shapes of his pectorals with their twin patches of hair revealed; down go the khaki pants and the boxer shorts; and suddenly he's nude, his knobbiness and hairiness suddenly all of a piece, put in perspective somehow by the naked totality of him, his penis thick and pendulous against the heavy, dark-haired balls.

Then quick, splendor covered up again: the peculiar jock, rubbery and clinical somehow, big red shorts, shirt of slippery mesh, glasses; he's back to being ugly and nervous Mr. Kablutis. Well, maybe not *that* ugly. I cannot make any connection between his body and mine, not for the life of me: I am pudgy and pale forever, I hate the hair on my body, hate my body itself and wish to hold it back from any further development, any more strange flowerings it might choose, and at the same time I can't escape the fact that his body is a secret wonder, a troubling delight.

❧

My investigation of cool reaches its height when I plan a party, an act of social bravura. It is to be a Paisley Party; I have conceived the notion that it will be a stylish kind of fun if everyone comes wearing an item in that newly fashionable print. I make the invitations by hand, drawing large paisleys on cardboard and cutting them out to hand to friends at school. Roger and Mike, who are never separated from each other for fifteen minutes, despite the fact that it is universally agreed that they are All Boy, make fun of my invitations, but then they are not invited, and I can tell—surprise— that they would actually *like* to be.

I have made friends, in part because I excel at the game of Password, which we play in class in imitation of a popular TV show; the game involves giving another person associative clues, in order to get them to guess the word you're thinking of. I am nothing if not practiced at daydreaming associations to words, which have to me the sensory actuality of colors, the materiality of texture and of weight. The kids who *are* invited actually all come, including a girl named Trudy Bisbee, whom I've proclaimed as my girlfriend, so entirely unthreatening are her clutch of wiry blond hair, her rhinestoned cat glasses, and her homemade dresses. It is a real party. I serve punch and chips on the picnic table I have covered in butcher paper decorated with the squiggly shapes to which the event is dedicated. I have wrapped our back patio—just a slab of cement, really, with a roof supported by four redwood posts—in filmy translucent plastic, and on it I project one of my light shows, shapes drifting around while the slide projector smokes and the portable phono plays the records my friends have brought: "In a gadda-da-vida, baby, don't you know that I *luhhhv* you. . . ."

❧

Suddenly we're moving again, back to Tucson, for whose heat and clarity and light my mother's been longing these years. End of cool; it's been something new, to know the same kids for two years, to form an identity and then actually begin to change it. I have never before been able to blossom, or at least reinvent myself in a social light. But my parents are energized, their anticipation contagious, since there's more news than just my father's transfer: his doctor declares there is nothing untoward in his lymph system, nothing at all, which a second opinion confirms. Miracle cure? Or evidence of a misdiagnosis in the first place? Was it ever there? The burden of the diagnosis, the bodily costs of his therapy have wearied and taxed them, leaving them shaken, but that's behind them now, maybe forever, and we're all going back to the place where my mother was happiest, and this promises that the sunlight of her good spirits will warm us all.

8

Valley of the Moon

Our new house in Tucson, on East Rosewood, is built of burnt adobe, the facade completely covered in a variegated ivy my mother loves. A deep-yellow wall in the living room brightens an interior weighted by the dark bricks of the fireplace wall. *Brighten* is also what my mother seems to do, as if her will were rallying after a series of dim years. She decorates the house with a new sort of nostalgia: up goes the old print of the hunting dogs in their sepia field, as always, but now they're joined by plates of a weepy transfer design called Flow Blue, and an antique clock whose pendulum measures out the minutes, filling the house, regular pulse of our days.

On weekend mornings before it's too hot she haunts the Swap Meet, a flea market held in the sun-dazzled parking lot of an old drive-in: acres of chipped china, colored glass, musty books, *Life* magazines: evidence of history, in Arizona, where there isn't much.

She buys turquoise bracelets, their blue a bright watery sea color, more saturated and vibrant than the cool blue of the china, and wears them against her darkening wrist. She plants a plum tree and a feathery jacaranda, and commissions a wrought-iron gate for the garden, curlicues framing an old central panel of iron artfully scalloped like fish scales, an architectural fragment from a Spanish monastery.

Relations are resumed with Helen Doyle, who's going on alone at the Hacienda, though since Mr. Doyle's heart has failed, Helen's own heart is not quite in her yarns and stained glass and copper enameling. After a year or two of stumbling through her grief, she has returned to her consuming plan, the building of her new Arabian quarters on the other side of town. Now her gallery holds unfurled blueprints and a cardboard model of the villa-in-the-works, which seems half hacienda, half Alhambra. Art lessons resume. My mother joins a group which paints the still lifes Helen constructs: peaches, a black Oaxacan pottery bowl, a mandolin. I am brought along for lessons, too, but what is it I want to do? Ceramics, glass, jewelry? I can't quite settle on anything, and don't seem to have the patience for craft.

I decide on glasswork, assembling pieces of cut and broken glass, melting them in a small kiln, just hot enough to fuse the pieces together into ornaments one might hang in a window. I make a strange, spiky-looking bowl by hollowing a form out of soft firebrick, then firing found bits of broken glass inside it till they sag together into something rounded albeit slightly threatening. I enjoy this tinkering until one day a visitor to the Hacienda, a European professor whose wife is also taking painting lessons, examines my work and says, "So there is no intention to what you do, no craft? You merely put things together and see what happens, by chance." There is nothing I can say to that. I feel bored, restless; there are great things inside me, surely, but who has the concentration or skill to bring them out, and how to choose where to begin, when any gesture eliminates other possibilities?

My mother seems bored, too, a little rebellious. One day she's had enough of the limes and the mandolin, and whips out a long scrap of watercolor paper and a bamboo-handled Japanese brush and paints, quickly, in thick spontaneous strokes of ink, five Chinese horses running across the field of the page—something like what she used to draw on her precious pads of paper when she was a girl? But Eastern now in their simplicity, each animal made of the fewest possible strokes of the brush, each line alive with energy: rebel horses, free, a little angry. It's the best thing she'll ever paint. Then it's back to the lesson.

For my part I clean the bits of firebrick off my bowl with muriatic acid and a scrub brush; the blue-green form emerges, chunky and provocative like some inventive piece of modern Finnish glass. We display it atop the stereo, under the heavy, swaying pendulum of the clock, but I haven't counted on the inherent tensions within the different densities of glass, and in a few weeks the whole thing flies apart, all by itself, without anyone even touching it, since it had only momentarily reconciled the forces it contained.

~

I am myself a walking example of contradictory forces barely held within one troubled, adolescent frame. Suddenly I'm six feet tall, my boyish fat reduced to mere pudge. But I'm nowhere at home in my body, in large part because I am consumed by desire. Of course I'm bored with my crafts and my schoolwork, incapable of commitment, since inside I am seething, my lusts hotter than the kiln. That's my body: a stiff insulating container for my desires, an armor for holding that potential conflagration in check.

I understand that my desires are unacceptable, and likewise undeniable, and therefore their forbidden nature seems to fuse with their power, the two somehow inextricable. I cannot escape the dual need to enter into my fantasies and to censor them at once, a condition which affects my sexual daydreams in this way: when I masturbate I think only of men, but I don't let myself see their faces, just parts of bodies—chests, thighs, the swell of a bicep curving into a dusky nest of armpit. The fantastic, partial bodies blur and meld, and are reflected in a little collection I make for myself. I've never seen pornography, at least not involving men, but in catalogs and magazines there are sometimes pictures of men with their shirts off. The public eroticization of the male body is years away, and might as well be light-years; my budding erotic life would have flourished, given the likes of Calvin Klein underwear ads! I find scraps of male flesh in the back pages of the Sears catalog, and I cut out the bodies—losing the heads in the process—and save these bits of men in a hidden envelope, where the pectorals and bellies are both lovely and oddly remote, entirely lacking in context.

My high school's huge, fluorescent, anonymous, and whatever promising gestures I'd taken in the direction of cool back in California have collapsed. This role's more familiar: outsider, new kid, nerd, which here makes for a comfortable if unrewarding invisibility. Lunch is the worst: unstructured time during which you must take your cheeseburger and fries and shake from the snack bar and figure out where to sit. These safe-looking fat boys, the periphery of this group of studious girls? Over there, where there's no one sitting? Oh, pray for an over there.

Praying has entered into my daily routine now, specifically when I go to the locker room. I pray not to get an erection there, on the cement benches, confronted with the display of undress. In fact, it's wildly unlikely, since I am so nervous in the jostle of naked boys I can barely breathe. I look straight ahead and hold myself stiffly and seriously as if to say, *these images will not penetrate me, I am entirely indifferent to this scene*; often it's true, and I am, since the pale and pimpled ranks of fourteen-year-old boys can seem unlovely. But there are those images which do register, when I sit on the bench tying my hateful regulation sneakers and pulling up my hateful striped crew socks and suddenly look right into the passing revelation of some naked, athletic boy. That boy's body and mine seem fixed in our separate realms, no commerce between us, no real resemblance. At home, tonight, I'll unfold this image secretly, longingly, but right now I'm bargaining with God, asking for my dick to stay small. I bargain all the time; I say, *tonight I'll think about a woman, if you try you can. If you think about women sometimes then you're okay. Think about a woman once, and then you can think about men three times.*

I'm a disaster at football, soccer, running, gymnastics, and especially climbing ropes. Softball's less dreadful, since I can dream away the period in right field, at least till I miss some fly ball and the earnest boys start yelling. Wrestling's not so bad, since my size means I am inevitably paired with fat boys, who have even less strength than me, but then there I am, pinning some inert kid who's given up, holding to the mat his sad, yielding weight.

The coaches make matters worse; uninterested in helping me gain access to physical activity, they actually take an opposite tack, shaming me and other hapless boys as a way of bonding themselves to the rest of the class. They underscore their masculinity, their common strength, by pointing to the failures of the fatties and the girly boys. I can see clearly that the coaches are themselves nervous boys, proving a point, but I'm powerless to do anything about it but keep my resentment in my face, limit the degree of my participation, and get as many excuses as I can: sore throats, bad coughs. The fat boys and the sissies are made to do jumping jacks, to run laps, though some days they just give up and have us keep score. The strong boys, the coaches' favorites, go off by themselves and lift weights, talking among themselves about the knowledge they hold in common. Coach de Sade stands at the tiled opening to the shower, at the end of my hour of tribulation, making sure that each boy has stripped and lined up, checking off our names.

These hellish days seem unrelieved, so I make of home a refuge: I choose paint colors for my bedroom, absorbing myself in the process, picking out brushes and roller, holding paint chips to the light: dusty sage, like the natural dyes I boiled out of desert leaves years ago, for the walls; a dusky olive for woodwork and bookshelves. I'm going to wrap myself up in someplace private, marked with evidence of myself; my own pictures, and books and magazines, my own music, some incense, a beaded curtain from the import store, my hidden treasure envelope of parts of men. If I have to spend the day with those idiots, at least I can have someplace nice to read.

∾

There isn't much peace in the rest of the house, however, not since my grandfather's come to live with us. I don't know where he's been these years, but the old man—Orlin, my father's father—arrives in Tucson on a Greyhound bus, carrying two ancient monogrammed suitcases strapped round with leather belts to keep them shut. His clothes, in the bright undifferentiated light of Arizona, make him seem ghostly: battered gray fedora, scarred cane with a yellow rubber tip, a vest of some kind of boiled wool felt worn over collarless shirts. When he changes clothes, I see his undergarments, scratchy-looking amber things with buttons and plackets; he's a revenant of the nineteenth century here in our spare room, right off the dining area, where my mother used to keep her painting supplies. Now it's Orlin's room, and in no time he seems to have filled it with an aura all his own, as if the old country world of East Tennessee has suddenly been recreated, in microcosm, just behind our yellow louvered doors.

Orlin rocks in an old green rocker, reads his Bible bound in black leatherette, and writes letters in a shaky, spidery hand on blue stationery he's brought with him, in one of the cigar boxes in which he carries his treasury: old fountain pens, rubber bands, paper clips, stamps, and most precious of all, his tobacco. He loves snuff as he loves—as far as I can tell—nothing else, and the yellowish brown juices of the stuff seem to have seeped into him like some kind of insidiously pervasive tea: his teeth, his fingernails, his skin, even those weird antique underclothes all seemed stained by an essence of tobacco dissolved in spittle. Which he produces in vast quantities, so much so that he requires a coffee can beside his rocker, and since it's a lot of work for him to get up and make it down the hall to the bathroom, he urinates in the can as well. The resultant noxious mix ferments, over the course of the day, until he carries it to the john and commences making a new batch. It takes precedence in any space he occupies, his signature, his spoor. It isn't hard to understand why his other children—my aunt Marguerite, my uncle Clarence, his favorite—have had it with him, why he's been packed up and shipped out on the West-bound bus.

My mother's horrified. I am, too, though since I have no responsibilities in his regard I can slip away more easily. She's responsible for his dinner and his laundry, which must make even a strong soul quail. When he doesn't come to the table for a meal, my mother brings him his dinner on a tray, but sitting at the dining table we're all aware of him eating in the next room, or refusing to—he doesn't approve of my mother's cooking. The fumes of his coffee can slink around the dining table like diabolical incense. The tension and resentment in the house are palpable; my poor father seems to think he has no choice but to take the old man in, but my mother's so angry about her new occupation that her vile mood seems to loom as large as Orlin's.

I think if she felt any shred of tenderness toward him these tasks would be lightened, but her old histories with him seem bitterly fixed despite the straitened circumstances of his age. As for me, I don't feel much for him because I can't form any sense of a character beneath the cranky surface at all. I don't seem to exist for him, and I am far too much of an aesthete, at fourteen, my sensibilities too delicate to go investigating who he is. I've seen him, through the half-open louvers, changing the undergarments, seen him, in fact, masturbating, an ancient man bent over himself, intent, on his pale back the skin cancers blooming in black profusion—melanomas, like my father's? His body's a disaster, but somehow he seems indomitably tough, resistant, fierce. He's a murderer, after all, who lived for years on squirrel.

∾

My mother comes into my room, reeling, upset, possessed by some information she can't contain. I put down my book (Oscar Wilde's *Salome* with the Aubrey Beardsley illustrations? *Auntie Mame* or *Little Me*? I've become a veritable expert at scouting out anything in the library with a whiff of the lavender about it, a detective fueled by need. I've found an amazing book of beefcake photos of bodybuilders called *Here's Power for You*, pornography disguised as exercise, but that's for secret perusal. The overdue fees accrue.) She says, *You don't know what's happened, I can't say it, it's terrible.* I say, *What?* She says, *It's too awful to talk about it.* I say, *What?* And she steadies herself as if she were nauseous, as if even to utter the words made something actual to her, something she doesn't want to be real. But she can't keep it in, either. She says, *Your sister*—intake of breath, eyes turning to the wall—*has had an abortion*.

And then she turns right around to face the little bathroom adjacent to my bedroom and vomits into the sink, her response that visceral, as if the idea of losing a baby were enough to send some tremor through her flesh that she couldn't control, wrenched as she is in body and soul.

I don't get it. I'm a little excited by the thought of my sister doing something so transgressive, but I don't really understand why it's so horrifying, why does my mother find this so unthinkable? It seems to me she doesn't even like children, not really; oh, she sentimentalizes the babies we've seen along the highway south of Nogales, the beautiful Mexican kids for whom she brings along tins of cookies when we take a trip below the border, and she likes to send gifts home with Alicia, who comes every week to vacuum and scrub, little presents for the *muchachos* with their darkly gleaming eyes. But something about it makes me nervous—because these children are in fact remote from her, romanced in some fantasy of a simple life? Exotic, their physical beauty enhances her idea of their virtue, their unsophisticated goodness, their unquestioning and admirable faith. Or maybe I judge her too harshly. Do they stand for the grandchildren who seem to be lost to her? Perhaps it's simply that Mexico isn't so far from the East Tennessee of the 1920s: a rural, deeply connected family life she remembers and can't have again, though she's chosen to flee it, though she hated it, too. Don't we always want it back, a little, the old life we've run away from?

Though our latest encounter with that old life has proved entirely disastrous; some irreparable *contretemps* between my mother and Orlin has happened while I am at school. By evening she is refusing to go on, refusing to. My father and Orlin have words, the old man waves his cane threateningly, and before the night is over my father's called Uncle Clarence, and after dire and absolute refusals Clarence has agreed to take Orlin in, at least until the old man can be placed in a nursing home. Miserable tension, the next few days, my mother tight-mouthed and quiet. She brings the old man trays of grits or tapioca, which he refuses to even look at. The ancient bags are packed again, bound tight with their leather straps. Orlin puts on his traveling clothes, including a tie which must have seen World War I if it's seen a day, and my parents drive him to the bus station. Returning home, my mother opens the spare room, thinking after a few days of airing she'll reclaim it as her studio, and then she finds what he's left for her, coiled in the green vinyl seat of the rocking chair: an extraordinarily large pile of shit, even more fragrant than his signature musk of urine and tobacco juice. Before it's cleaned up, she makes sure that my father and I have both seen it; she wants witnesses.

Faith, or at least the desire for faith, is part of the reason my mother responds so viscerally to Sally's bad news. We've joined a new church, Saint Michael and All Angels, an Episcopal congregation whose ritual goings-on are as near to Latin Catholicism as the absence of a pope will allow. We have been various sorts of Protestants: Presbyterians in Tennessee, according to family alliance, Methodists in Tucson later on because there was a church nearby, mild and tepid with its grape-juice-and-cracker Communion and suburban angularity. For years we've been nothing at all.

But now Saint Michael's is a school of ritual, liturgy, and style. The priest of the church is a handsome and flamboyant political activist, with a flawless sense of aesthetics: the church is adobe, sand pink, all curves and archways, set in a grove of twisted old olive trees out of van Gogh. Every Sunday the vaulted apse is pierced by Bach fugues on the organ, and clouds of frankincense billow from the swung silver censors. Father Fowler collects antique vestments, so each Sunday's procession displays this season's beaded and embroidered albs and surplices. The statues are Mexican, antique, the flowers arrayed in bronze and lustrous black pottery: perfect, for what my mother wants, which is something like the abdication of self in ritual. A form of simplifying oneself? Here it is possible to step out of the contradictions and doubts, the tensions that make things shatter from within like my unfortunate bowl. Here she can immerse herself in what she can actually believe in, which is beauty.

Father Fowler himself, with his groomed white beard and raptorial dark-eyed gaze, is something of a beauty, a fact lost on neither my mother nor myself. He gleams with the allure of conviction. He projects a fierce quality of certainty.

I am, indeed, smitten by it all, if not quite convinced, since at fourteen I find it difficult to embrace something my parents like. But it's all undeniably gorgeous, and I am captivated by the confrontational edge of the priest's politics. He works for Cesar Chavez's grape boycott and organizes picket lines at Safeway. My mother seems essentially indifferent to his moral messages (the necessity of confronting our racism, civil rights, charity), but utterly enraptured by matters of style. She covers her head, when she enters the sanctuary, which Episcopal women are not asked to do. Her collection of mantillas swells. Piety, in fact, seems a kind of performance; new phrases pepper her vocabulary: *Lord help us and save us, Saints preserve us*. It's as if she's doing a kind of imitation of someone more certain than herself, someone whose faith emerges from a history so deep and continuous there is no question of choosing whether or not to believe. Such women, the women whom she's decided to be, in her lace headpiece and her discreet crucifix, don't have abortions, and neither do their daughters.

And of course it isn't simply the depth of her feeling that actually makes her vomit when she pronounces the word "abortion." I haven't learned to recognize what's going on, though I will soon. I haven't thought about how most trips to the grocery—where she's befriended the owner of the store, an Arab American who greets her lavishly, the mornings she drives the three blocks to the Star Market—yield a bottle of vodka along with the Whip 'n Chill and Rice-A-Roni, the cheap cuts of beef to be tenderized and braised all afternoon to produce her Swiss steak. Not every time, not every day. But increasingly her behavior's taking turns toward the dramatic. She's "fainted" in the kitchen more than once, and she sweeps around now and then, head in the air or held broodingly low, clearly in the throes of some drama she's enacting, some old conversation, some play which is taking place silently, though it leads her sometimes to audible weeping.

M a r k

D o t y

∽

When she's composed herself and turned back to me, I ask her how she knows. She says she and my father grew suspicious, because Sally asked them for money, three thousand dollars for a new roof. Why they doubted that, I don't know. Her marriage had broken apart, her Jerry smitten with a woman he'd met at the evangelical church he'd joined. *Saying "Amen" in the choir*, my mother tells me, *but all the time with his eye wandering*. Sally had told them that part, how she'd been on her own for months, struggling to raise her three kids, but they'd hired a private investigator to find out the rest.

A private investigator? My mother's narrative slips into the realm of the movies, a fevered *noir*. And as in all such tales, if you go poking into what you don't need to know you won't like what you find. How did they think a single woman with just a high school diploma took care of three kids, in 1966, in Memphis, Tennessee?

∽

Many years later I will love the stories Sally will tell me about her high life in those troubled days—or low life, depending on your point of view. And I think she'll love the stories herself, as people with flamboyant Pasts often come to do. Not that you want to live like that anymore, mind you, but what energy and delight lie in narrating those bad old days! And don't the tales get richer, more deeply worked over time: the wild highs higher, the scrapes narrower, the past gaining a glamour polished by distance and the wonder of having survived it all?

Whatever the detective found out sent my mother into a tailspin, but when I learned these tales—too shocking for my mother to tell me herself—they seemed episodes in a mid-century *Fanny Hill*. In this chapter Sally turns a trick with a senator, and during his postcoital nap scoops up his wallet and credit cards and heads right for the Fontainebleau Hotel in Miami Beach; in those pre-computer days, stolen credit card numbers took weeks to catch up with you, and of course she knew precisely how many weeks to stay. In this chapter she hangs out in Memphis with her friends Sam the Sham and the Pharaohs ("Hey there, little Red Ridin' Hood . . . "), and exacts revenge on some rival with attitude when she and her girlfriends add to the haughty girl's gas tank a couple of pounds of sugar. She winds up visiting the apartment of a folksinger who's come to town to soak up Memphis blues, "Cute, though he couldn't sing worth a *damn*: Bob Dylan, did you ever hear of him?" In this chapter she steps in front of a city bus, timing it just so as to get knocked flat on the asphalt, then settles out of court for six thousand bucks. She has a weekly liaison with a mortician, whose erotic requirements are quite precise: she arrives at the funeral home, changes into a shroud, and powders her face a very pale shade. Then she lies in an open casket and tries to hold absolutely still, breathing as little as possible while he takes his pleasure. Comic relief: she gets a job in a carnival, working as a Snake Lady, half woman, half boa. This is how it's done: Sally sits in a wooden box like one of those individual steam baths in an old movie, just her head sticking out. There's a rubber coil wrapped around her neck, and from beneath the coil emerges the long, thick body of a real snake, whose head is concealed in another compartment of the box. When the people pay their quarters, there she is, the Snake Lady, wisecracking, her red bouffant gleaming, and her work is to talk back to all the smart-ass customers with something funny to say. I do not think my sister incapable of embellishing a story, but this one's true; I know because she still speaks "carny," an incomprehensible secret lingo carnival workers use to communicate without the "straights"—the yokels and townies—knowing what they're talking about. Carny is an amazing variation on the idea of pig Latin, with variable numbers of nonsense syllables inserted before consonants; it sounds like insane glossolalia, brush-tent Baptists high on Jesus and strychnine.

I think these stories entrancing; how could anybody who ever wanted to run away think otherwise? My mother must want to escape herself, is in fact devoted to practices of escape, but for her my sister's wild days are horrible. For her some vista opens out— downtown blocks, pawnshops, cocktail bars, Negroes, as Robert Lowell put it, "with curlicues of marijuana in their hair"—which isn't anything like what she must have wanted for her daughter's future. These same elements strike me as exotic ingredients of a vivid demimonde nothing in all the environs of Rincon High School seems to match. My mother's anxieties are a brew she probably can't sort out herself: shame, humiliation, a will to control what that girl does, a rage that she can't control much of anything, a bitter wish to stamp out her own wildness: Chinese horses brushed on a scrap of scroll, then put away. Moral outrage? The shock of having your daughter turn out to be somebody you don't know? The plain fear that her child will come to harm?

Not entirely unfounded, since soon the police catch Sally with some checks and some prescription pads, some bottles of pills that can only have come from the drugstore she entered the hard way, through a hole she and her friends had cut in the roof.

∾

Like my mother, I'm also smitten with a priest, or a priest-in-the-making, anyway. In my new drama class I've met a boy two years older than me, a thin Polish Catholic named Rudy, with high cheekbones and a lank fall of black hair combed up in an oiled wave—shades of Jerry Lowell! It must have been his exoticism that drew me first; his family had moved to Tucson from the East, and something about his pale skin and dark hair, his white cotton shirts and black slacks and the holy medals he wore under his white T-shirts, gave me a little thrill of difference.

It wasn't his body, exactly, though I liked his wiriness, the white, thin reach of him which I associated, somehow, with litanies: *tower of ivory*. In fact I never even allowed myself to imagine sex with Rudy, which was just as well since he was a straight boy as well as a future seminarian. He was himself devoted to a girl in the drama class, a cool and brilliant blonde named Veronica Roberts, whom he loved with a noble idealization after the fashion of courtly love. He hadn't any intention of giving up his vocation for Veronica; she served him more as a sort of hobby, an aesthetic object. And so I attempted to model my passion for Rudy on his idolization of her, imagining him as an ideal figure, a boy who'd give up his pale and denied body for the higher life of God.

Rudy and I would take holy field trips together, visiting a big pink church on Campbell Avenue, where nuns prayed day and night, in four-hour shifts, in front of a rayed gold monstrance in which the Host was displayed, going to Catholic bookstores to look at prints by Sister Mary Corita (WONDERBREAD, her red letters proclaimed above big floating spots). Without exactly thinking about it, I infused my new religiosity with my ardor for Rudy, right to the point of abandoning Saint Michael and All Angels with its liberal sense of social responsibility and becoming Catholic myself. I joined Rudy's anonymous, modernist church with its sad statues and cheerful new felt banners across the street from the shopping center on East Twenty-second, a church with no noticeable politics at all. Conversion was weirdly easy: a few classes, a baptism, the uncomfortable and hasty experience of a first confession. Are you troubled by lustful thoughts? Nothing to worry about. Now, did I feel different now?

What I'd expected, of course, was that I'd feel closer to him, more Rudy-like, but it doesn't work. I thought there'd be less of a barrier between us. I envision us as chaste brothers, impossibly close in our joint aspiration toward grace, helping each other in the progress of our faith. But in fact I think he's moving farther from me, nervous about our friendship. One day he and I go to the large ugly church to pray. I'm mad at him, he's holding me at a distance, I want—something, I don't know what—and before I even think about what I'm doing I've slipped from my pew onto the cool terrazzo of the floor. I've fainted, or I've pretended to faint? I've gotten his attention, anyway.

I am my mother's son.

⤳

Word from Memphis comes back slowly, in bits and pieces; my mother doesn't tell me what my sister says when she calls from jail, where she's awaiting trial, or about what her lawyer says, or much else. I overhear a little, and try to picture a world I can only imagine in little fragments of image: green uniforms like hospital scrubs, bars, rough sheets pulled across thin mattresses, women with scrubbed faces bartering for a little makeup or a hairbrush.

That summer, the hot months after my freshman year in high school, I take a volunteer job working for Project Head Start, in the old barrio downtown. I get up early, when the streets of our neighborhood are still, and walk under the rinsed blue dome of the six A.M. sky, the moon paling in the first flush of desert dawn. I walk the eight blocks to Speedway and catch the bus there. I don't mind getting up early; there's something appealing about the silence, waiting for the bus alone, riding down the long strip of fast-food places and shopping centers. Past the movies and the car lots, past the old adobes around the university, with its rows of olives and palms, into the warehouse district, the gritty edge of downtown.

Head Start's a chance for preschool kids to play, listen to stories, practice whatever the teacher thinks important, which in this case involves learning the names of things in English: numbers and colors, body parts, and articles of clothing, drills in following directions she turns into elaborate games of Simon says. She is blond, rounded, kind. Every child in the class is Hispanic. My job is to follow the teacher's instructions; I am her adjunct, but I come into my own on the playground, which she doesn't like much because of the heat. I love it; I am to supervise and to play along and to talk with Antonio and Mercedes, Lourdes and Guillermo; they like my glasses and my long legs (good for hanging on to), my curiosity about them and my let's-see-what-we-can-do-now attitude. And they like that when we walk across the street each noon, to a public school lunchroom where we're fed on pink plastic trays, I am forever passing my tacos or half my fishwich or my beefburger-on-bun-with-dill-pickle to these skinny, endlessly hungry little boys. I'm not supposed to do this—Head Start rules—but their need is irresistible; there's no mistaking the reality of their hunger.

One day the teacher's planned a field trip. A bus chugs outside our little cinder-block classroom; we are going to the Valley of the Moon! I've never heard of it, but the teacher says it's a tradition, a place kids have visited for years, and she's been lucky to get us an appointment.

We are carefully organized; each child has a partner, whose hand she or he is to take once we arrive. We're instructed to stay together. I've been assigned to Antonio, who at just five is the biggest, rowdiest boy in the class; he's eager, self-confident, and capable of being obstreperous. We sit side by side on the bus, which crosses Speedway and then heads north into an undeveloped area of desert I don't know. Pavement gives way to dirt roads, houses to flat open land marked by creosote and greasewood, an occasional jackrabbit shooting out in front of the wheels. Just when we've turned enough times to confuse me thoroughly, the bus pulls up beside a chain-link fence, idles a moment, coughs to a stop. The kids look out the window, confused but willing: *Is this where we're going?* In truth there's nothing to be seen but the bit of fence, and a narrow dirt driveway, and a hand-painted sign, in drippy white letters, that announces VALLEY OF THE MOON.

We file out of the bus, line up with partners, the teacher at the front of the line, then the double cordon of children, Antonio and I in the final position. We wait, and in a moment there's a figure coming our way down the narrow drive. He (I presume, though in fact the body's so completely hidden that gender is just a guess) is dressed entirely in black: black boots and some kind of Western slacks, a black shirt, black gloves, and—most strikingly—a wide black hat from which descends a black veil, dense enough to obscure the face entirely, falling from the brim of the hat all around his head, all the way to just below the shoulders. He draws close, raises a gloved hand in greeting, and announces, "I am the Mountain Gnome. Welcome to the Valley of the Moon!"

A little laughter from our group, but not much—mostly wide eyes, exchanged looks, small shoulders raised in a gesture that means, *What is this?* A little shivery fear commingled with delight.

The Mountain Gnome instructs us to follow him, and turns and begins to walk back the way he's come, talking all the while. He says that he is the discoverer and keeper of the Valley of the Moon, which is for everyone but especially for children. He says we are to leave all negative thoughts, all sorrow and loneliness and fear, at the gates, for we are entering into a fairy place of love and goodwill. And soon we are passing through those gates, which are jutting, haphazard constructions of concrete in which the gnome's embedded bits and pieces of broken china, sparkly hunks of glass, weird bits of junkyard detritus—old Disney figurines, metal springs, any shiny thing that's caught his eye.

We follow along behind him through a twisty path of such assemblages—complicated, studded walls, open to the sky—steadying ourselves by putting our hands out to the narrowing, encrusted sides of the trail. We descend a few stairs, the path opens out, and we're in a broad sandy circle before the mouth of a cave. "This," the old man says (you can tell by his voice he's an old man, and his backlit profile when his veil falls between you and the sun), "is the fairies' treasury, where things are hidden for children. Scratch your feet in the sand and see what you can find."

The kids start shuffling, and sure enough, the sand is full of pennies. They shuffle harder and faster, pick up the coins, and the teacher urges them to slow down. "Can we keep them?" they ask. They aren't accustomed to being given money. The teacher looks to the Gnome, who nods gravely.

Soon we are moving forward again, this time up a curving stair along the side of a pathway of rock—hard to tell what's stone and what's painted cement, everything manipulated and assembled here, everything mosaicked and wrought, and little windows keep opening up in the stones along the way, in which lit bulbs shine on scenes of fairyland: dwarves mining their treasure, girl sprites bent under the weight of their chipped wings. Here Snow White, in a china figurine which must date to the day when that movie was new, bending forward, wide-eyed, breathless, her hands on her dirndl in front of her, as if she's confronting the newest and strangest thing in the world.

The path crests, begins to descend again. "Quiet now," says the Mountain Gnome, "for we are entering the Enchanted Garden, high, high up in the Valley of the Moon." I can't think how the old man's built the Enchanted Garden—for everything here is his handiwork, and it all has the same eccentric look, a signature style which says he's done it all alone, worked for years to build this fairy grotto. The Garden is a rounded opening, quite deep, in the center of a sort of hill built of cement and who-knows-what; its shady, rather dank interior is lined by seats the Gnome's carved out along the circular wall. In the center is a little pool, mossy and opaque, home to a fat and somnolent goldfish. In a wire cage sits a lustrous black mynah bird, sleek and imperious, who opens his beak now and then to squawk, or cry *Hel-lo*.

We sit in the niches in the sloping wall, or on the stony floor of the Garden. "Whenever you are troubled," the old man says, "send your thoughts here. You can travel out of your body—you know this, don't you?" The children look intent; they have passed no judgment. "This is astral travel: send your thoughts here, to the Enchanted Garden, where there is always peace."

We sit a moment longer; the bird shifts his weight, cocks his head, lets loose again.

And now it's up the path, through a thicket of creosote and mesquite, and suddenly here's something we haven't seen: a building shaped like a circus tent, only it's made of scraps of wood, bits and pieces of old signs and sheet metal. Inside are a double row of bleachers facing the dust floor, and a wall of pictures—photographs of fairies perched on the fingertips of Edwardian girls, snippets of old paper dolls, every sort of thing that must for the Mountain Gnome mean childhood, some timeless and strangely antique realm of innocent wonder. I understand that he's made every bit of this privacy himself; this is an act of preservation, of recapitulation, generous and oddly self-enclosed at once; his work is beautiful and peculiar, which is the only genuine kind of beauty, because it is the only personal kind: idiosyncratic, hard-won, like no other. Here he will perform for us the Magic Show. And it *is* magic: a wooden Tinker Bell slides down a wire and pops in a burst of light and smoke. Many silk scarves appear from ears and pockets, are cut and rejoined, tied in knots, then suddenly extended to amazing lengths. A snake emerges from a hat, a long, dull black snake which the children who want to—Antonio first among them—are allowed to touch. When the Gnome opens a little wooden door—where did it come from?—a pair of white doves burst out explosively, and Antonio grabs my hand and leans forward, just like that statuette of Snow White, breathless, completely absorbed in the show.

When it's over we clap and clap, and the Mountain Gnome bows solemnly, then leads us back to the bus. From somewhere-or-other he produces a stack of cards, and as each child files by he places a hand on the girl or boy's shoulder, with a tenderness that has a certain ecclesiastical air about it, a gesture of blessing. He gives each of us a card, a white business card in the center of which is stitched with red thread a single scarlet sequin. Underneath the bit of shine, the text reads: THE KEY TO THE FAIRY TREASURE HOUSE OF HAPPINESS, HIGH HIGH UP IN THE VALLEY OF THE MOON.

On the way back to school—where a sack lunch is waiting for us, not enough to feed this ravenous boy—Antonio and I hold our cards to the sunshine that comes and goes in our window as we turn the desert corners, trying to catch the light.

∿

In a decade's time the Valley of the Moon will go unvisited, the desert all around built up with new subdivisions, only the old man's fenced lot untouched, his towers and caves of cement and chicken wire crumbling. This dereliction seems inevitable, both because of his age and the age in which he found himself, too late in the century for fairy palaces in the desert on the edge of town. And then some high school students will find him, kids who themselves remembered a childhood tour; they'll find the Mountain Gnome sick and half starved, living in one of the unheated caves of his strange Hobbit-house. A sort of coalition will form for his assistance, and it seems only moral justice that he dies with some sense of the gratitude he's engendered, from a lifetime of his own peculiar gift-giving. The Valley of the Moon is there still; you can visit it, and though not much of the Gnome's handiwork has lasted, some sense of possibility, a whiff of strangeness lingers, conveyed perhaps by the sense of how much this place meant to those who've preserved it. Though it would be hard now, looking at the mere physical remains, to understand quite why it moved them so.

9

Samson in the Temple

Drama class is my high school's haven for the odd and misbe-
gotten, the dreamy and peculiar. Under the stage lights, in the
workshop or at the makeup mirror, we turn out to be possessed of
gifts no one could have foreseen; we turn out to be somebody after
all, down in the Drama Department, which feels like a separate
world from the rest of Rincon High School, squirreled away in a
basement corner, darker and cozier than anything else in those
acres of linoleum and fluorescent lights.

My sister's life has taken a turn toward trouble—a trial, a prison
sentence, Jerry given custody of her children—and home's begun
to feel unmoored, unpredictable, but I'm enjoying the beginnings
of a resurgence anyway. (Can you have a *re*surgence, when you've
barely surged at all?) I let go of Rudy, or he of me, and suddenly I
find I don't have the least interest in Catholicism, except for the
lives of the weirder saints. (Saint _____ , whose name has slipped

into a dark crevice of my memory, irretrievable, although the fact that she lay on a wooden board till violets sprouted and bloomed beneath her mortified flesh rightfully granted her immortality; Saint Christina the Astonishing, who died for an hour, then returned to life, only to find the smell of human flesh so revolting that she had to fly to the rafters of the chapel to escape the mortal stench.) I'm finding my way toward some kind of social acceptance again, a certain degree of cool, in Mr. Frakes's realm.

Mr. Frakes, the prince of our theatrical zone, is one of those rare teachers of young people who have no interest in holding power over anyone. He is courtly, self-possessed, consistently well mannered in any circumstance. Dapper and donnish in rimless glasses and salt-and-pepper hair, he has such an obvious respect for intelligence and creativity that it startles me. I have never met anyone whose intellectual life is so democratic: he likes ideas themselves, not just his idea. He likes the arts, not merely his art.

His overriding passion is for the theater itself, and he assumes that anyone who's entered into the little city over which he presides (black box theater, dressing rooms, workshops, warehouse of old props) shares his passion, or wishes to. This assumption amounts to respect; what we do is collaborative work, our common shoulders turned to the play at hand, which is sometimes tired and crowd pleasing (*You Can't Take It with You* or *Dark of the Moon*) but more often something Mr. Frakes loves: Beckett, Anouilh, Shaw. We can't do Sam Shepard (too much profanity) but we do—unheard of in a high school—Jean-Claude van Itallie and Megan Terry, the new plays of the hour.

And so we find our way downstairs, to him and to one another, the kids who belong exactly there, the ones too thoughtful and idiosyncratic to find their place upstairs or, God forbid, in the gym. We're the kids who seem to carry our inner lives right in front of our faces, and in the Drama Department it is suddenly just right, just perfect that you live in your interiority. Here we prize strangeness; one of the new words that enters my vocabulary is "bizarre," offered as a compliment, in admiration, an all-purpose assertion of praise.

I've begun to shift my style. Out go the smoked plastic glasses, replaced with sharp new oval wire-rims. And I've taken to avoiding or refusing haircuts, and have arrived at a stylish length like the Beatles on the cover of *Sgt. Pepper's*, and suddenly I'm getting it: I have a new status in the eyes of my peers, I'm a person whose opinions and interests matter. It's the beginning of sophomore year, and I'm in Advanced-Placement English, reading Fitzgerald and e. e. cummings. A new English teacher—bearded, hirsute, all that body hair somehow like an expression of his simmering nervous energy, as if he's literally *wired*—has us pull our desks into a circle and discuss Ferlinghetti poems (I dislike them even then), as well as give ourselves our own grades. We think he's ridiculous but entertaining, and he's fired in about three weeks. No matter, we go on with *The Great Gatsby* anyway; my new glasses, it occurs to me, must resemble the pair of spectacles on that spooky sign mounted out on Fitzgerald's Long Island dunes.

Something new's happening. I am relaxing into myself, tasting what it's like to approve of myself a bit because other people do; if you're a cool kid, then you're not a sissy, at least not till fourth period, after lunch, and the daily forced march to the locker room. We're creating a new category, in our school, my friends and I, a social niche to serve as an alternative to soshes (yellow windowpane plaids, canvas belts) and cowboys (stiff Wrangler jeans, white T-shirts) and hoods (greased or ratted hair, eyeliner, black leather). Or rather, we're absorbing something that's happening out there in the wider world, an emergent category of otherness. We're about to be what we'll call "freaks," and some of us couldn't be happier about it; the label denotes a stylish, desirable otherness. Heaven only knows how many of us, downstairs in the drama club, were young homosexual men and women; that aspect of ourselves simply did not come under examination, was not made visible in our new category. A freak, by definition, wasn't a sissy, wasn't queer. It was a form of liberation, strangely, this new place to dissemble, the best place yet to hide. One day I solidified my new fame by going to school in a shirt I'd made myself, a simple dashiki cut from an Indian block-printed cotton bedspread in a soft print of yellow and orange paisley shapes. Simple, you just cut out two pieces and stitch them up by hand with a needle and thread. Voilà: a new world, heady, its horizon nowhere in sight.

So it doesn't matter so much if my mother's drunk some afternoons when I get home from school, or if my parents spend evenings sitting on the couch as if locked in some long, intricate conversation they can't seem to find a way out of. If she's been drinking a lot her sentences begin with "Face it, Larry . . . ," an opening salvo followed by some unpleasant truth about him, or me, or my sister, or all of us. He listens, defers, she persists. He tries to argue with her, then gives up and defers some more. I try not to listen, try to steer clear; it's better if her attention doesn't turn to me. But there's a persistent rhythm to her voice, a kind of edgy litany which seems to pervade the house, and the longer it goes on the more my father seems to punctuate it with low sounds of assent, "That's right, yes, that's the way it is." I can hear in his voice he doesn't mean it, but he seems compelled to agree with whatever she says anyway, required to placate her. They're fixed in a kind of combat on the green Naugahyde sofa, though it's a strange sort of battling, since they are not arguing; she is railing away, wearing him down from disagreement to deferral, night after night. What are they wrestling with there, why doesn't someone get up and walk away?

One night I'm called into the room, and she begins to criticize me for something—that I've become affected, because of my drama class? That I never clean my room? Something she says pushes me too far and I snap back, and in an instant my father's up off the couch and coming at me. He says, "Don't you ever talk to your mother like that," his fist in the air, raised to strike. In an instant it occurs to me that now I'm as tall as him; I've never noticed this before, our bodies are the same size, and here he is about to hit me. I step back quickly, and something strange happens; he is so involved in the momentum of the swing that he falls right to the floor. And there we are: my mother lying on the couch, my father at my feet, facedown on the gold carpet, and me standing in the doorway, not knowing what to do with myself, suddenly self-conscious, without a clue what to do next. My father lifts his red face up and says, "Get out," and I do—past the plum tree and the dusty olives, out to the still-hot twilight of Rosewood Street, the mountains going deep lavender in the distance, off to any place at all.

One day—rare moment of rebellion!—my father takes a pair of pruning shears and has at the ivy that shades the front of the house, the thick and tangled vines my mother loves. It's full of birds' nests and spiders, glad of some respite from the Tucson sun, but he doesn't care; there is no limit to his pruning. When he's done the exposed fired red adobes look naked and raw, hardly a vine scrambling up the wall, and on the gravel beside my father's feet is a huge pile of leaves, glossy in their cream-edged dark greens. When my mother sees it she starts to cry, a silent and recriminatory weeping that goes on for hours. My father busies himself in the carport and the tool shed, oiling the clippers, working with a certain combination of trepidation and pride. He's struck back, in some way, but the victory is so small, so tangential to the real, unspeakable war between them, that it can't seem like much.

~

After a bout of drinking she's rigid and remorseful, mouth tight, her head down. She says nothing at first, then eventually lets out some self-recrimination which doesn't attempt to hide its undercurrent of hostility: "You couldn't forgive me for what I've done." Silence. The iron moves, the dish is wiped. "I'm the one who's sinned." The more she drinks, the more she's invested in a kind of spiritual economy, a moral accounting—as if what struggles in her isn't the desire for vodka (for obliteration? for freedom?) but forces of good and evil, which wrestle out their drama on the darkened stage of our house—our kitchen, our couch, our dry garden. But the struggle seems unwinnable; she has always just failed.

It is in such a mood that she goes to visit my sister in a Tennessee State Prison, where Sally, brilliant survivor, is getting by. I don't hear much from my mother about the experience—taking a plane to Nashville, a bus to some little town, going through security, being led down some painted concrete corridor to the visiting room where her daughter's on the other side of a partition of glass. Or is it more casual than that, the two of them sitting down at a cafeteria table together while a guard in the corner watches them and the other lucky women with visitors? I'll never know. My mother's assumed a sort of martyred look; in memory I cast

Loretta Young in her role now, nunlike, self-consciously good, eyes downcast in sorrow, then turned up to heaven. That moral rigidity again; you're either pure or fallen.

All I know is Sally's in occupational rehab, learning to make false teeth. She's gaining weight on the starchy diet in there. She's sent me a wallet she made for me, woven from thousands of cut and folded green cigarette packs and their cellophane wrappers: an intricate prison craft that takes forever, a cross between tramp art and origami. The design of the cigarette packs themselves is obscured by the folding, but you can tell by the colors that my sister has been smoking an awful lot of Kools.

❧

Is it my mother's idea, the haircut, and my father gives in to it, in order to placate her, to protect himself from her wrath? Has she hectored him till he agreed, in their nightly battle on the couch?

Or maybe he won't have his son looking like that, the man towering next to me; suddenly I don't seem as tall as he does anymore. What does long hair mean to him—woman, hippie, fag? My hair is an embarrassment, out of control, represents trouble, they are ashamed to be seen with me like that. Does it have to do with seeing longhaired kids on the news, feeling disturbed by the politics and trouble their tresses represent?

Or maybe they're not going to let another child go down some bad path, some thunder road, because they've lost one that way already.

Whatever the case, a decision has been made, and my father simply bullies me into the car, although I am weeping unashamedly. I have said in every way I know that I don't want to do this, that it isn't fair, that my hair isn't even that long. And of course I can't explain, since I don't understand myself, what my hair means to me: I can't articulate the way in which my look represents the outward sign of a dawning social possibility, how it signifies I'm becoming *someone*. Anything I can say is to no avail anyway; the issue here's no longer hair.

I'm hauled to the barbershop. I've been happy to avoid them, these male rooms with their smells of cut hair and machine-oiled clippers, floor wax and blue disinfectant for combs, their copies of

Argosy and *Saga*, magazines whose covers bear antlered deer caught in the sights of rifles. I won't cry in here, but I won't talk either. The barber knows exactly what's going on; he plays something like this scene every day. He talks to my father, not to me, and my father sits in the spectator's seat, not even bothering to read a magazine, involved as he is in watching my disgrace and submission. I'm shorn bare as the front of our house the day the ivy was cut away.

I don't say anything to him, don't say anything at home; I go to my room and close the door, and I don't even go to my bathroom mirror. I've seen enough in the barber's glass; I don't want to see my head, which I know is ugly, which I know has lost any shred of dignity or the style which had begun to make me somebody besides the pudgy out-of-it nerd I've been all my life. I get into bed and stay there, though it's four or five in the afternoon; I take off my clothes and under the covers I am a big shorn baby, a naked ugly boy, and I try to do what I do sometimes, a kind of spiritual exercise. I pay attention to each part of my body, starting at my toes, and I tell it to relax, to let go. By the time I'm up to my chest I am moving into some other state of mind, dreamy, loosened. When I think of my ruined head I try to place that thought far away from me; I am relinquishing, am nothing but relinquishment. When I reach the top of my head I go back to my feet and start over, and this time I discover I can let go even more. And if I'm lucky I can begin to leave my body altogether—as if I were one of those strange saints, freed of the stinking burden of flesh, which won't do what it's supposed to, which can be shorn till it's nude and unrecognizable. Now I can cut free of it altogether, and I feel myself lift from myself, start to float up out of the confines of my skin, unmoored, buoyant. I am moving toward the bedroom ceiling, and soon I am face-to-face with it, not my flesh-and-blood face but my soul-face. I'm weightless, a shadow, uncapturable in my phantom form. And then I turn, spirit-body that I am, to look back at my bed, at that abandoned boy empty there, his pale scalp glowing in the twilight. He looks like someone no one wants. I don't either; I have no use for that awkward form.

And then he's up, after a while, out of bed, when he knows his parents are asleep, and he goes quietly to the kitchen, where he knows his mother keeps a bottle of sleeping pills. Only Sominex, not exactly an efficient poison, but they're what's at hand, so he shakes them out and stands at the sink with dozens of white tablets in his hand, looking at the little white discs, each incised with a line down the middle like an aspirin. He hasn't turned on the light; he holds the pills over the sink, and they're lit by the street light outside shining onto the carport and the silvery roof of the parked Dodge. He pours a glass of water and swallows the whole bottle, in a handful, all at once.

∾

I cannot quite, now, put myself in the place of that boy, that stupid, fourteen-year-old boy, shorn to a military severity—humiliating in 1967, and exactly the way I wear my hair today. Now a body seems so precious to me, so embattled already. Dramatic boy, he doesn't see how dangerous it is to make a point with your life. (Had he really wanted to die, I suppose, he would have; certainly under the sink were the ordinary household chemicals that would have done the job. But he didn't think of them; does that mean he wants to live, finally, or just that he doesn't want to suffer? I cannot tell you; I can't read him that clearly.)

Doesn't he know hair grows back in a hurry?

But it isn't about hair; nothing to do with this haircut is about hair. For the parents this is one thing they can control, when everything else is going awry; for the father it's one way to get that harpy off his back, and she's right about this one anyway.

But for the boy hair is power, too, or rather seems to grant him access: a way to be a person people might like, a way to be seen. (Little ripple of memory: pictures of Samson in Sunday school, oiled and spread-eagled, a muscle man chained to the columns of the temple, writhing like Steve Reeves, his beautiful shorn head the emblem of his sexual defeat.)

Hair was a defense, too: a way for that mistake of a boy not to be seen. He wants that so desperately he'd die for it.

Or kill? Suicide's a misplaced homicide, most of the time; that boy's rage is immense, and unthinkably dangerous, since he's also utterly dependent on the people he's coming to loathe.

And there isn't any way, not that he can see, to get away from them.

And this is what they want of him anyway, isn't it, what he deserves? At the core he thinks nobody sees, at the root of him, where no air ever reaches, what he is is something to be ashamed of.

∾

Even a full bottle of Sominex, it turns out, doesn't kill, but it makes you thoroughly crazy. (Or maybe, in fact, the pills didn't have that much to do with it. Sominex is mostly aspirin, and perhaps I was just ready to go a little crazy, maybe I didn't need that much help.) I'm told my parents heard me moaning and babbling in the night, and could not wake me, and then tried to take me to the hospital, though I held on to the refrigerator door and called them every filthy name my chemically enhanced imagination could come up with. They thought I was having a bad trip, the sort of thing they'd read about, and the hospital strapped me down to a bed and put me in the care of a burly male nurse—an aide big enough to restrain a psychotic, hallucinating six-foot-tall kid—who wasn't to leave me alone for a second, not even after I woke the next morning. Everything was glowing, strangely pretty, the walls and curtains and hospital bedding luminous, ultraviolet, as though I were seeing colors outside the normal range.

I couldn't remember a thing after I lay down in my room, my hands crossed on my chest, ready to throw my body away. Nothing of my apparently Herculean thrashing and my wild tongue. My father waited thirty years to tell me I made a pass, under the influence, at the nurse. Or the nurse said I did; my father doesn't question the claim, though to me it doesn't seem likely; I wanted to die (or, more precisely, to disappear, which isn't exactly the same thing) more than I wanted to have sex, which I had not yet been able even to fully *imagine*. But who knows how will and libido flare, self-control shut down by sleeping pills? Maybe I came close enough to the end of my life to know what I wanted most: another body, that consolation for the grief of having lived which resides in the skin of another. Maybe I didn't want to die without touching a man first. In my own experience, it seems that coming close to death—our own or someone else's—brings us just a hairsbreadth from desire.

I soon prove calm—I *am* calm, strangely so, as if I have quite forgotten my hair—and am released from the leather restraints which hold my hands down to the bedframe. My friend Bill from drama class comes to bring me some books I ask for; I'm still half in my radiant state and he looks wonderful to me, delightfully funny, and I babble away while he looks at me with raised eyebrows and not-too-well-concealed amusement. Bill's brought my sketchpad, full of the comic strips I like to draw, which are silly little sketches influenced by R. Crumb and the new underground "comix." My nurse asks to take a look. He holds the book away from him, his big hairy arms poking out from his green hospital shirt. He scans the pages and pronounces them revelatory. "These say a lot about

you," he says. "Are you homosexual?"

In my post-Dionysian bliss I'm unrufflable, so I just say, "Yes."

"I could tell by these drawings," he says. Even in my blur I don't get how my comics reveal me, so he explains that all my male characters have noticeable nipples. (Maybe it seems a stupid explanation because it *isn't* the explanation, but of course he doesn't say anything to me about the "pass," which maybe happened, maybe didn't. And perhaps I'm just part of a regular night's work; how many gay kids who tried to kill themselves wound up in that hospital ward?)

He says something that's supposed to indicate he's my friend, someone I can trust. He asks if my parents know and I say no. He says, "You can have a decent enough life, you know. Not a normal life, with a family, but you can have a life."

I'm still coming down to earth from the free-floating realm of the sleeping pills, but this is sobering me quickly. I've never talked about this before, not with anyone; I don't know what to say. He wants me to confide in him but I don't feel quite safe; something about his offer of friendship feels deliberate, or professional? Or maybe it's because he keeps mentioning his wife.

Then he tells me there's a homosexual man who works in the hospital, another nurse. "He keeps it quiet," he says, but he'll ask him to come and see me.

Which he does, that evening, a neat blond man in his twenties, in his hospital scrubs, so clean as to be self-effacing. Memory preserves this scene as though it had been filmed through a lens smeared with Vaseline: soft focus, blurry at the edges, all its gestures ambiguous. He stands at the foot of my bed and fiddles with my chart, playing with the chain which holds it to the footboard. He says, "Hi." He seems about as awkward as I am.

I say, "Hi."

We don't know where to go from there.

He says, "How are you?"

I say, "All right."

Silence.

I say, "How are you?"

He says, "Great."

What am I supposed to do? I don't have any way to get at what swirls inside me; I am so scared of myself, really, that I don't feel there *is* anything inside of me, just a blank place, emptier than the hospital room. I have no questions; my sense of anything my life might be is tiny, inchoate, buried beneath a great weight. Where would I start to talk to this man, the first gay person I've ever met who actually says he's a gay person? *Does* he say it—to me I mean? I don't even remember.

There is an idea, in contemporary physics, that time branches out into multiple dimensions, that what doesn't happen in one world may happen in another, as all the possible outcomes of any gesture fan out into a wave of possibilities. This moment, in my hospital room, is a kind of crux; if he and I could actually have talked, how might my sorry present and my uncertain future have changed? Suppose he had said, "God, I used to feel just like you"; suppose he had told me how much silent company I actually had, how many kids felt exactly the way I felt. Suppose he told me how he'd come to breathe more freely, how possibilities opened for me like those multiple realms, worlds I couldn't even see yet. Suppose we talked about our common sorrow till we could actually laugh about it, till I could imagine that sorrow as something which might *end*; suppose he had just told me to have patience, that the loneliness and sorrow of gay kids is just something to be lived out.

I imagine the effects of any of those statements as plainly earth-shaking, an unthinkable openness. I envision it like this: the lid of the box of myself sprung, no more constricting sense of being sealed off. Air come rushing into the tomb, fear brought into the light and shown for what it was: a shadow, a mistake that didn't need to persist, a sorrow which could pass. Years and years open out differently, and my story writes itself in another, freer hand.

But that moment doesn't take place, not that way. In 1967 the doors are locked, the exits sealed; I can find no route away from shame. The talk we're supposed to have flounders, since neither of us knows where to begin; the possibility of connection sinks before my eyes, as if an ocean liner were passing out of sight before you had the first idea where it might be headed.

He looks at the floor, fiddles with my chart. Then he says, "Tomorrow you get to go home."

10

Wear Your Love Like Heaven

The astonishing thing, in retrospect, is that no one ever says, *What were you thinking, Mark? Why did you do that?* Much less suggest that perhaps it would be a good idea for me to talk to someone.

(What do I think those men in the hospital could have done? They tried, in a rather bold way for the time, to reach out to me, and yet when I think of their gestures all I can feel is a heated, steely anger. "Decent enough?" "Not normal?" An awkward silence in a dark hospital room? Couldn't we do a little better, for a boy who's just swallowed a bottle of pills?)

Perhaps it's that the nurse's tale—an amateur expert's conversation with my father, perhaps with both my parents?—has told them all they need to know. Maybe it's that the idea of a counselor, a therapist, is so far outside their experience it doesn't ever occur to them? Or is it just more trouble, what's happening to me, a boiling brew of it, and there's no room in their already turbulent household for such attention?

Whatever the case, my parents settle on a remarkable strategy. They not only do nothing, they effect a policy of Leaving Me Alone. Hair, clothes, friends: leave him alone. Hours, whereabouts: likewise. It takes me a while to understand what's transpired, the loosening—the abdication—of limit. It's as if I've been cut adrift, in a way, in my freedom: I can eat and sleep in their house, most of the time, though I start looking for friends' houses where I can stay when I need a respite. This new adult prospect—go where you want, where would you like to go?—brings a kind of exhilaration with a funny note of sadness in it, as if in my excitement I sometimes barely notice a feeling like the floor slipping out from under me: who knows, just now, where I am?

∾

Maybe you know a little place you can go to
Where they never close—Downtown.

The actuality of downtown Tucson doesn't seem like what Petula had in mind: empty storefronts with soaped windows. The Greyhound station, where sorrow and trouble have soaked right into the varnish on the scarred wooden benches. A sad pawnshop (INDIAN JEWELRY!), repository of the lost treasures of the poor. Fading department store where nobody goes anymore. The movie theaters I loved as a kid are mostly gone, too, except for the seedy and dangerous Lyric, where once the luminous Beast from the future enthralled me. Now its screen is patched with tape and gangs of tough kids from the nearby barrio my father's helping to bulldoze for a new civic center hang out in the aisles, spoiling for a fight.

Downtown's the province of the drunk (the ones who lack what my mother has, someone to shelter them) and the destitute. Of course there's a gay life there, blossoming after dark, but I don't know it. Maybe it *is* Petula's promised place, but the scales on my eyes keep me from seeing. I don't know how to see, and would be terrified if I did. Though I am perfectly clear, deep in myself, about my wishes, I can't imagine translating them into action. Afraid of being seen, of seeing myself as I am, I spend most of my time somewhere above my body, at a remove from desire; I will not acknowledge what I know. Alone in my room it's another story: I can sink into autoeroticism as into the warmest and most thrilling of seas, give myself over entirely to the delights of flesh. And even though I don't think my body beautiful, it is capable of such absorbing elation, of occupying me entirely.

Then I button myself up, stuff pleasure back down in its place, become the head on a stem I am, floating above my flesh, deeply disloyal to my body, and go—well, not downtown, but to Fourth Avenue.

Fourth Avenue's a strip of low storefronts near the university, and here cultural change has taken on its visible, public form: retail. Here's a bookstore called the Hungry Eye, which has so few books that they are displayed face-out, singly, on wide shelves: Ginsberg, Krishnamurti, Anaïs Nin, slender volumes of surrealist verse illustrated by haunting collages, *Whole Earth Catalogue*s and back-to-the-land handbooks and heaps of pamphlets and newsletters and homemade books with swirling shapes on their covers, a visual meltdown frequently involving smoke, mushrooms, wizards, and Volkswagens—the signature vehicle of the era. Later, on acid, I'll ride over the Rincon Mountains in my friend Dino Gordon's yellow Volkswagen and actually hear the vibrations of the car perform Rimsky-Korsakov's *Scheherazade*, the entire thing, while I lie in the back seat and watch the desert sky through the lovely biomorphic shapes of the Beetle's windows.

But I get ahead of myself. I haven't discovered drugs yet, though they are one of the determinants of Fourth Avenue culture. Why else does the bookstore offer prisms and kaleidoscopes, and little cubes of colored plastic which serve as the stash boxes of choice? In the Hungry Eye I read the poems of Federico García Lorca for the first time: *Verde, que te quiero verde.* The language itself seems saturated in color, better than the bright boxes, a deep coppery cistern verdigris: *Green, I want you green.* Sensuous and mysteriously exact, translated from Spanish of course, but somehow not translatable into everyday speech: evidence of possibility.

Fourth Avenue is in fact a trove of evidence, new ways to live. There's the macrobiotic food store, with its tubs of miso and scary-looking umeboshi plums, and tales of cures effected by the proper balance of yin and yang, contagions banished by brown rice. The art cinema's movies are British, Italian, other. The sandal shop custom-crafts their wares, and in a burst of feeling flush—my father's slipped me some money for clothes and shoes for school—I order a pair of sandals, Roman centurion style. The sandalmaker says I've got the longest, skinniest feet he's ever seen, and three days later produces a fabulous product: they're flat soled, and sport thick straps which crisscross up my ankles, inevitably calling up associations with Galilee.

∾

I plan to leave altogether, to hitchhike to San Francisco for the summer after the Summer of Love, 1968, with the notion that I won't be back anytime soon. I am going to a city of loving youth who will build a new order founded on peace and freedom. I love that cheap song on the radio, with its odd electric poignancy, its quality of sadness so overt beneath the invitation: "If you're going to San Francisco, be sure to wear some flowers in your hair. . . ." It's a kind of revision of Petula Clark, but I cannot hear then how much more cynically knowing it is, just under its promise of hope and change.

I've written farewells in my friends' yearbooks, at the end of sophomore year. My parents drive me to Los Angeles and drop me off on Highway 1, the Pacific Coast Highway, a fact which seems now to demonstrate the Leave-Him-Alone policy at its most bizarre; I don't remember anything of the drive at all, not even who was in the car—some vague echo of memory wants to suggest my mother drove me, alone, but can that be true? I am divided, I think, between my anticipation of adventure and something else, something unspoken underlying my conscious excitement, which is this: it is one thing to run away, and another thing for your parents to *help* you run away, to aid you in your going, which is a form of abandonment.

I make it to the Bay Area in only two rides; in between them, I scramble down a rugged Big Sur slope to study a tidal pool in the chilly half-fog: a yellow sea anemone opening and closing its fist of ribbons; starfish; cold, cold water. I remember a passage from

James Joyce I read in my favorite bookstore: "He was alone and close to the wild heart of life . . ." That's how I feel, at fourteen, solitary, and glad of it, I think, and near the edge of more than these sea cliffs.

Once in San Francisco I don't know what to do. I don't know what I expected, exactly. I walk up and down Haight Street, looking at posters and the cheap kaleidoscopes and more of those little colored plastic boxes, stuff to play with while you're tripping, but I don't seem to connect with anybody here. The song they're playing everywhere in the Haight is Donovan, "Season of the Witch," a moody, edgy ballad about—what?

> You've got to pick up every stitch,
> Two rabbits running in the ditch,
> Beatniks are out to make it rich—
> So strange—must be the season of the Witch.

I love the clothes—shawls and sarongs, beads and bells—on the hippies I see on the street, but all the faces look guarded and closed, tired; at home my new look helped me forge some connection to people, but not here. I'm a tourist, an amateur. In the afternoon I go to the Fillmore Auditorium to hear Country Joe and the Fish. There aren't a lot of people there, a little throng of dancers near the stage, couples and solitaries scattered here and there around the big dark room. The band looks anemic, their pallor lunar. I sit cross-legged on the floor, my duffel bag beside me. A little ways away there's a man dancing alone in a beam of black light, which illuminates some Day-Glo paintings, a scatter of swoops and swirls on the floor. He's rocking, shifting his weight from hip to hip, and then he's completely still except for his head, which is doing all the dancing; he looks utterly alone in all the world, turned on, sealed off in his own vision, blissful but oblivious, emblem of his age.

Out on the street, someone says, "Hey, would you like to come to a Buddhist meeting?" and I am relieved to have something to do. The meeting's upstairs in a crowded little apartment. We face an unrolled scroll with a single flower in a vase before it and are taught to chant in Japanese: *Nam Yo Ho Renge Kyo*, which means: "God is the Jewel in the Center of the Lotus which is My Heart."

We're told to wish while we chant, for anything we want, and not to be embarrassed about wishing for material things. Happy Buddhists give testimony, in fact, to how they wished for nice cars and good apartments and got them, then realized those aren't the things that truly satisfy. I wish for a place to sleep, and sure enough as we're filing out of the room a guy who looks like a longshoreman, a white-haired and red-nosed fellow in his fifties, asks me if I need a place to crash.

"It's not much," he says about the floor of his room, "but you can have it." I'm grateful for it, and spread my father's scratchy green army blanket out on the wood and wait to fall asleep while the longshoreman snores in his single bed. It takes me a long time to sleep, tired as I am; I am thinking of the Buddhist chant, saying it to myself while the biggest cockroaches I've ever seen scuttle across the floor. In the morning my gray benefactor tells me I have to get better at the nomad life: "Your duffel's too heavy," he says, and he's right. I've brought the things I thought I needed for the Summer of Love: a few books of poetry, my new tarot deck, that homemade dashiki, my best hand-patched jeans.

I walk to City Lights Bookstore in North Beach with the heavy duffel. I sit in the basement and read *Siddhartha* by Hermann Hesse, cover to cover; I love the part where Siddhartha sees the river of human lives and faces, every visage like a bit of foam, a ripple on the surface of one water, all of it streaming onward through time, ancient, always new, never still. Back on the street, adrift, I suddenly feel completely like what I am: fourteen, too near the wild heart of things. I don't have an inkling about how to take care of myself, where to go next, what to do. I call my parents from a pay phone, and I can tell they're relieved to wire me the money for a bus ticket home. When my mother picks me up at the Greyhound station, I know that she's actually glad to see me.

∾

I'm not sure if she's so glad to see my sister, who comes home—comes, that is, to my parents' house in Tucson—on a sort of early-release program, a furlough from jail which is intended to prepare her for life on the outside. She's been dosed with Antabuse and released on my parents' recognizance; it seems surreal that she's not allowed to visit her children, who Jerry's keeping away from her back in Memphis, but she *is* allowed to bring with her a girlfriend from prison, Jenny, a lean, wiry butch with a fine but nonetheless pronounced black mustache. My parents are wildly uncomfortable, the household fairly athrum with alarm. I don't see much of my sister, since I quickly scope out that it's another good time to get lost, though I love when she tells me about how to survive in jail. The best tip is to ask frequently for a psychiatric evaluation; tell them you think you're losing it. When they give you the word association test, employ the following responses: Red = blood, Black = murder, Green = money, and then the clincher, White = ghost. "White = ghost" will get you a nice rest in the infirmary any time.

The official purpose of the visit is for Sally to check out jobs, look for an apartment, start to get set up so she can go back to the parole board and make a good case. But she and Jenny are ready for some fun, too, and thus ensues a bitter evening's comedy.

My parents head out to a fancy Mexican restaurant, La Fuente; I'm invited, but I attempt not to go anywhere with them now, since I know what will happen, and I'm right: my mother has too many whiskey sours, sings with the mariachis, gets offended by the waiter, feels too full after the meal, and decides she's going to stretch out and take a nap on the restaurant floor. Meanwhile, Sally and Jenny have been out to some clubs, and they've decided, why not, they'll bring someone home, a pretty Latina, and just as they're all proceeding to have a little party in the living room, who comes home but the parents, fresh from a scene with the restaurant staff. Horror and pyrotechnics; good thing I am safely away, drawing comix with Bill, hanging out with Dino and listening to the Rolling Stones, but once I'm home the shock waves are still reverberating. Sally's packed off back to jail, and that woman—well, we don't plan any further mention of her name.

The scene is taken as a major assault on piety, which indeed has come home to roost in a new way. My mother has been banished from the Altar Guild at Saint Michael's, the club of women who wash the vestments and arrange the flowers; she's more or less incapable of either task these days, and doubtless an obstreperous presence, too. Her disbarment is a terrific blow to her.

She goes to one last Sunday mass, wearing her ecru mantilla, but before the service ends she's out the door, into the courtyard, climbing the gnarled trunk of one of the old olive trees. When Father Fowler and his attendants arrive at the door, after their procession from the altar, and the people start to file out, blinking in the sunlight, there's my mother, sitting on a branch and shouting her imprecations at the hypocrites. "Face it," she cries, "O ye of little faith!"

I don't go to church with them anymore for the same reason I don't go along to restaurants. My father tells me about this later, after he's brought her home. Is he laughing while he tells it, shaking his head?

Returning to church is out of the question now, but she isn't done with it yet. A few nights later, while my father's sleeping, she gets up in the middle of the night and goes out of the house, barefoot, in her nightgown, and begins to walk toward Saint Michael's. I imagine it's cool, the air alive with crickets and locusts, she's gliding in the diaphanous white gown past gravel lawns and sprinklers spinning over grass, past clusters of creosote and cacti; then the sidewalk runs out and she's walking in the road, crossing the arroyo that makes this end of our street impassable in the rainy season, down and then up again, walking the two miles of East Rosewood across Wilmot and then up to the church gate, through the olive grove, scene of her shame, to the church doors. Of course they're locked, and this scene you must imagine performed by Vivien Leigh: she's pounding at the church doors and weeping, she's crying to be let in, her feet bleeding, and she'll continue till the police come.

Sleepwalking, my father says. My mother buys a large statue of the Madonna, Oaxacan pottery made of black volcanic clay, unglazed but polished to an anthracite sheen. The new icon sits atop the television, and candles burn there day and night. The thwarted Catholicism of my mother's childhood blooms into icons, and our house fills up with images of the Holy Mother: Mary with her feet on the moon, crushing the head of the serpent. Mary decked in blue cloth covered in stars, just like the Donovan song, with its droning keyboard, that gliding vocal trance: *Wear your love like heaven.*

I hang out in Himmel Park, halfway across town, happy in the spontaneous gathering of other kids like me; there's always somebody there, but on Saturdays it's a sort of festival: field of patched blue denim, smoke of incense weaving in the air, little bells tied to handwoven sashes, sewn to backpacks and bell-bottom jeans. There's a band that'll play for free, if we can get up the cash to rent a generator. I smoke my first joint in the basement stairwell of a dark apartment building on Speedway, where I've stopped while I'm walking the miles home from the park. Someone's said, "Hey, you want to turn on? I'll lay this joint on you." I am expectant, thrilled, but I can't decide if anything happens at all: are those streetlights brighter, those headlights sparkling? Next time, smoking a pipe full of dope cured in opium, no doubt about it: suddenly I am loose with laughter, the tension in my body uncoiling, as if I've a thunderstorm in me, blue-black rainclouds moving up my spine, beautiful, full of promise. Driving around in the desert with Dino, we stop on some dark turnout off an unpaved road to toke up. Dino's parents are well-off; they live in a beautiful Hacienda Bellas Artes–style casa, shady archways around the blue tile of the pool, and he never seems to lack for resources. His parents won't let him grow long hair, but he sports emblematic round wire-rims and a Guatemalan poncho woven in twenty shades of sheep. He likes me, I think, because I'm distinguished from his other friends by my what-the-hell attitude: *show me what I won't do.* His other friends, the kids he's grown up with, who live in his neighborhood and are expected to go on to Good Schools, conduct themselves a bit more carefully, but I'm hell-bent for the next experience. He cures his dope in hash, then burns it in a pipe of tempered glass whose liquid chamber he's filled with Drambuie. One night we look up from our dedicated inhalations to find a saguaro owl sitting right in front of us on the ground, appraising us, half his six-inch height given over to his enormous eyes.

◠

Now begins a kind of blur, in memory, a swirl, shadowy on the edges, whose primary elements are my mother's inebriation and my own.

I've planted the seeds culled from a lid of grass in a large Mexican flowerpot, thinned the sprouts to the single strongest, and grown, in the sunny window of my room, a resplendent six-foot marijuana plant, the picture of radiant health, its buds and flowers waxy with resin. I inform my parents that it is a Mexican bean. I take great care with the harvest, which is potent and enormous, my own private shoe box full of dope.

It is each afternoon's solace. I come home from school after I've dawdled as long as I can; some days I have to literally step over my mother; her mock fainting's become a regular ritual, and you can't always tell if she's pretending to have passed out or has just chosen an unlikely place to rest. Sometimes she waits to see if someone will come to her rescue; sometimes she gets upset and cries out, "I fainted, and you're not even going to come and pick me up!" but other times she just drifts away, a little respite. Her tries at cooking grow stranger. One day she's trying to fry some chicken, putting the cut-up parts of the bird in a bag and shaking them in Shake 'n Bake. But she's forgotten to close the bag and there's floury stuff and chicken everywhere, pieces of chicken in the drawers, in the corners of the kitchen, where they'll stay for days. She painted the avocado cabinets herself, with little flowers and flourishes of scrollwork, when we first moved here, but those seem like ancient days now, and the painted flourishes look tired and tentative.

Every afternoon's after-school joint makes the tension in me spread out into a sort of glimmery horizontal. I go to my room and pull out my stash, and from the first good deep hit I begin giving myself over to it entirely. I like to go for a walk then, in the heat, and feel the parallel between the inside of my head and those heat-mirages coming up off the pavement. Nothing's too clearly outlined, nothing too sharply delineated.

Or I like to stay in, sinking down into my body, looking at my envelope of pictures, or the dirty book I've found at the drugstore. But sometimes, afterward, or even instead of touching myself, I'd rather just do my meditation exercise, trying to slip out of my skin and float away, a little boat moored on a long rope, loose enough to go free, awhile, on the tide.

I've given up on San Francisco for now, but there's still Fourth Avenue. At a combination clothing and record boutique, I've gotten a pair of silvery bell-bottom trousers, cuffed, subtly metallic, which I call my Flash Gordon pants. And then a pair of dull pink bell-bottoms, the color of bubble gum rubbed in ashes. Combine these with my thrift-store finds and my back-alley trash diving and I am beginning to achieve a look. I like jet beads, chokers, filigree rings in art nouveau swirls like the lettering on Alphonse Mucha posters, long scarves, satin, those ubiquitous Indian block prints that begin as bedspreads and wind up sewn in patches onto everything. A little patchouli oil, and look who you can be: a self-creation, playful, a little outrageous but very much of the moment, since I have been studying the moment very attentively. Liberating, these new clothes with their implicit message of freedom and experiment, expansiveness and liberality. I don't mind when someone yells at me from a car, calls me a "hippie faggot." They are, after all, talking about my *clothes*.

❧

I may spend every afternoon in a smoky cloud of my own making, but at school I focus, at least in drama. I've been cast in *Waiting for Godot* and I pour myself into my part, Estragon: slapstick, melancholy, bitter but with the hopeless élan of a survivor. Bill plays Vladimir, and we execute our dark vaudeville routines with the expert timing of friends who know each other's rhythms and patterns of speech exactly. My mother comes to the performance. "I didn't understand it," she says afterward, "but I understood it."

❧

When Sally gets out of jail for good, staying with us until she can afford a place of her own, we commence a new friendship, though in my aura of smoke and Beckett I must not be easy to know. My phrase of the hour is "far out." I'm a blurry young man who's doubtless a familiar type to her; she likes me but thinks, *Boy, are you ever* stoned.

With my new learner's permit I drive her downtown to the old department store, and she makes her first purchase as a free woman, a pants suit of a truly forceful purple. She wears it when I drive her back downtown, in the evening, to the Santa Rita Hotel, and drop her off just outside. I like to watch her walk away, an emphatic violet presence under her red beehive hairdo, strolling into the shadow beneath the pink adobe archway that leads to a bar where a girl can always make a little money.

And with that little money, she industriously sets to making herself a new life, finding an apartment out by the air base, moving out of my parents' house. She finds a job in a cocktail lounge, where she meets an air force guy, a mechanic with a limp earned from a piece of shrapnel in Vietnam, a man she really likes.

∾

Now I wish, sometimes, that I could see my mother's addiction from the inside, that I could look down that long tornadic tunnel as she must have, feel that pull that she wasn't ever strong enough to resist. I can't; addiction is one of those facts which resists comparison. You can't quite know it if you've never been there, since there's no way to say what it's like. In this way it most resembles sex and death, two experiences never—for differing reasons—adequately described. I want to ask her what she wants from it, what in those spirits so ultimately and entirely compels. But she couldn't answer that, could she, even if she were here?

Back then, at fifteen, I didn't want to know what my mother saw. I didn't see any connection between what she was doing and my own "experiments" with drugs—which is what they were called, in the parlance of the day. I didn't think my mother was *experimenting*; she knew what she got, when she swallowed her potion. If I thought about her booze I thought she wanted to close down the world, while my unpredictable powders and tablets opened it. I thought I was seeking something else in my spirits, too, some further understanding—entrance to the world above the world, or down beneath it? There is another reality, beyond this, isn't there?

On my first acid trip, half a tab of Orange Sunshine, the atmosphere broke apart into cubist planes of light and color, sound crystallizing in that air too, the world all made of lovely geometrics as in Cézanne, and I wanted to stay there. I am my mother's son.

∾

A thread links the life of art and the life of intoxication. Both are acts of self-enchantment; both involve the sense that one is linking one's life to a larger life. In my firebird dance—so many years be-fore—I'd felt freed of the constraints of a body I already under-stood as a source of shame. I felt joined to the music, which had a quality of purpose and scale about it, a context larger than any-thing I knew. Its depths were open, available, glimmering. And when you gave yourself over to it—put yourself into Stravinsky's hands, as it were—the circumstances of your life seemed to recede into the background: here, in the present, in the vascular pulse and hurry of the music, was everything that mattered.

With drugs it was, in some ways, the same. Getting stoned meant that the confines of awareness (here I am in the pressure chamber of my own body) seemed to loosen, and much of what it meant to be me, in the tired strictures of my own head, seemed to fall away. Something used to grip my temples, squeezing the sides of my skull, a pressure that had become so much a part of daily life that I didn't even notice it was there until grass or acid gently took the vise grip away, laid it to rest in a grassy field someplace. Awareness seemed to spread horizontally, my eyes opening wider, the membrane of my skin more porous and airy, the tension be-tween my vertebrae released so that spaces opened in my spine and I became taller, longer, open to clouds and rain, to the play of light.

The world one could participate in then was, in a way, an anonymous one, like the world of art—a current into which one might step, and find oneself identifying suddenly not with one's own body exactly but with the whole: *I am that streaming move-ment, that forward momentum.* Or rather my self's soluble, dissolv-ing in that unbounded.

But there was, of course, a difference. Art had a past, and a fu-ture; to dance or paint or write was to enter a tradition, a conversa-tion of human gestures across time. The masters went before, and pointed toward just how far there was to go. And what you made, for better or worse, might be here tomorrow. In the enchantment of intoxication, though, there's merely now: a grandiose feeling of immersion in what's larger than oneself, and no history, and noth-ing to look forward to. One is released from shame for an hour, two hours, eight, but somehow the falling back into limit is that much worse.

Perhaps it's that every time you enter into the life of art, you come back a little less yourself. This is not, I know, the going wisdom, which teaches us that art heightens our individuality, makes us more actual. But perhaps it's more like being dipped into a plating solution, or the way in which fossils form—a few cells carried away, replaced by something else. So that a gradual substitution is going on, a transformation or sea-change which has to do with conjoining us to a human community—or a once-human one!— quite indifferent to time: listen, pour yourself into the music or the language or the color, and now you are a little more Mozart, a little more Auden, a little more Holbein. Like fabric dipped into dye, to borrow a metaphor from Maharishi Mahesh Yogi, who used to say that the more we immersed ourselves in Being, the more of that transcendent state would color our everyday lives. Do we come back from the experience of art bearing in ourselves more harmony, more color, more of time?

If this is true, then every time you get drunk or stoned, reaching for a way out of the trap of the self through those magical agencies, you are, in fact, a little more yourself: stuck, limited, with fewer resources to climb out of the pit you sought to escape in the first place.

∾

Once, just once, my father actually intervened: he took my mother, certainly by surprise, maybe by force, and drove her to rehab. She hated it. Later she'd say she was mortified, because they put her in a room next to a heroin addict in withdrawal, and all that first night she had to listen to his screams. And she was mortified again when she went to meetings, the things people said about themselves, things she'd never say. Her addiction seemed to heighten her Southernness, as well as her Catholicism: *a lady would never say those things about herself.*

After rehab, repentance, rigidity: *you can't forgive me, no one can.* How long it was before she drank again—two weeks, a month?—I can't say; I was in the blur, I was in *Waiting for Godot,* and waiting for my father to protect me, or himself. He sat on the couch with her, listened to her tirades, and rubbed her back when she cried. Once he told me she had to drink, because of the pain of a pinched nerve in her back, pain she'd had since a suitcase fell on her from the overhead luggage rack in a train, in 1942. But he didn't want to talk much about it. What could he say, except it was better that I "lay low"?

That meant getting lost; my father would pull a ten or a twenty from his pocket and say, "Lay low for a while," and off I'd go: no plan in mind, necessarily, just a street kid's faith: what might the day shape itself to be? And where would the night find you, that creosote-scented Tucson darkness, warm and, if you got away from the spreading lights of town, gorgeous with stars? Anyplace at all and no place; everybody knows a kid like that, in no hurry to get home, always with one eye turned to the next: next meal, next friend, next place to sleep, next place to score.

I was getting good at "laying low," was becoming, in fact, resourceful. I carried my notebook everywhere, in a shoulder bag adorned with glass beads and old Chinese coins, a thick black sketchbook full of drawings and daydreams and fragments of poems—homages to Lorca, surrealist mutterings, wild rants. Nothing directly about my life—who wanted to write *that*? Or even could?—but dreamy and disjoint evocations of anxiety and beauty: smoldering guitars, swooning gardenias, constellations of my own devising.

My junior year of high school just beginning, I decided I not only couldn't face gym class ever again, but maybe I didn't have to. Between home and school was a new cinder-block doctor's office surrounded by ocotillos and prickly pear. I didn't think much about what I was doing; I just acted, as if I'd been planning this on some level less than conscious. I walked into the receptionist's office and asked to see the doctor. "Do you have an appointment? No?" She looked at me, taking stock. "Just a minute," she said, and left the room.

When she came back, she said, "Have a seat, the doctor will see you in a moment. Do you have any insurance? No? All right then."

The doctor's urbane, professional as he shakes my hand. He says, "Do your parents know you're here?"

"No."

Pause, thoughtful. "What can I do for you?"

"I'm a homosexual," I say, "and I need to get out of PE. I can't handle being in PE. I need a doctor's note that says I don't have to go."

He thinks a minute more, then he writes me a note. I am filling up with such gratitude I could cry, except that I am too numb to do so. I didn't know what would happen if I said it, and it's all right. It's all right. He says, "Have you considered telling your parents?"

I don't know if I even answer him, but my face must tell him something, and he hands me the note and tells me there will be no charge.

The note says: "Mark Doty is to be excused from physical education classes permanently." Period.

Dear Doctor Whoever-You-Are, this adult thanks you still, not for the note so much, though that's what the boy wanted, but for your acceptance, your tacit recognition of that kid's courage, or at least his nerve. You are a good man.

∾

And I've met another good man, too, a poet—unlikely encounter!—who's entered my life in this way.

I've enrolled in an acting class, at Shirley Raskolnikov's School of Dramatic Arts. Shirley R. is a somewhat blowsy British expatriate, given to pointy little high-heeled black boots from which she balloons upward into a generous frame, usually swathed in polka dots. The picture's crowned with a roostery shock of blond hair which proudly announces its divorce from the natural. She studied, years before, at the Royal Academy of Dramatic Arts, and indeed one of the things that fascinates me about her is the intensity and focus with which she pronounces the five-word name of her alma mater, the *Rroy-ahl ah–cah–duh–mi*, each syllable invested with a glamour only her carefully preserved London accent could reveal.

Classes meet in a wood-framed Old West style–theater in a clutch of buildings called Trail Dust Town, an approximation of a frontier village given over to restaurants and shops, places where you can get your picture taken in cowboy clothes. Shirley assigns improvisational exercises to us: *You have been presented with a bouquet of roses, and a bug in the flowers has flown up your nose. You are a machine designed to make children happy.*

Our task, for one class, is to bring something we've written ourselves and perform it. I memorize one of my poems and say it for the class, but Shirley says, "No, it's supposed to be something *you*'ve written."

I protest that I did write the poem. Shirley looks at me thoughtfully and says, "Do you have more?" I show her my notebook, and by the end of class she has formed an idea. She asks me to give her a selection of poems because she'd like to show them to a poet she knows, one who teaches at the university, who's published books of his verse.

It isn't long before the poet calls, and invites me to come down to the university to meet him. I go as if it's the most natural thing in the world, not feeling much in the way of trepidation, mostly curious. His name is Richard Shelton, and we meet at the Poetry Center, which is an old pinkish adobe near Speedway, surrounded by oleanders, a treasure house of books and tapes and magazines. Dick is probably forty, with curly red hair and a beard of reddish gold. He looks like a figure sketched on a vase by Picasso: there's a bit of the satyr about him, or the centaur. He's wearing leather sandals like mine and leaning back in a desk chair in a room papered with posters advertising poetry readings, and beautifully printed copies of poems signed by their authors in bold or tiny hands. He's completely personable and yet there's some element of the mysterious about him, too, as if some deep reserve of experience or knowledge were not quite available; the depths of him inform his surface but remain depths.

He wants to know where these odd and dreamy poems have come from, and he wants, plainly, to be of use. He doesn't criticize the poems much, offering an exclamation of encouragement here, a suggestion about word choice or phrasing there. He says I can use the Poetry Center's library any time; you can't check things out but it's open every day and has comfortable chairs for reading, and a universe of books, many of them extraordinary—letterpress volumes, hand-printed and hand-painted things, wildly exotic magazines printed in Florence or in Venice or sewn together by hand in the basements of Sausalito. Books of Kenneth Patchen's poems with covers the poet painted himself. He suggests things I should read, poets he thinks I might like who I'd never find on my own; many of them are the touchstone poets of his generation, people

I'm reading to this day: Merwin, Simic, Kinnell. I'm shy and hugely grateful. He invites me to come back next month with more poems.

In retrospect I can hardly believe my luck; out of the blue, exactly the teacher I needed has appeared, and he has the generosity to take time for a fifteen-year-old's groping poems and the wisdom to give me just enough, hold out some possibilities, and then stand out of the way. He doesn't try to shape what I do, merely points me toward what's possible.

Dick is a surrealist, or a neosurrealist, which is the fashionable mode of the day; he produces vast amounts of "automatic writing" and then culls from the random outpouring the images that strike him, forming incantatory poems which often value the life and color of images over the workings of the restrictive intellect. He believes in the wisdom of the unconscious, and the beneficent and tutelary powers of chance. (He is an avant-gardist, of course, but these principles seem to me now the signature faith of that age: the gates of Paradise are closed to those who seek them with the light of Reason.) He prefers the French pronunciation, *sur-ray-a-lism*; he reads French, and he talks about Breton and Eluard and St. John Perse. I've never met anyone like him; he's a walking introduction to another realm, himself a sort of Poetry Center incarnate in a human body, his erudition organized and directed by love, his passion for the art.

And in this way he's even a more powerful teacher to me, his identity more instructive than his advice. Poetry is the way he lives, the arts the element in which he moves. For him everything centers around the compelling power and charm of what people make. I visit his house in the desert, where he lives with his wife and son, who is a few years younger than me and plays a cello as tall as he is; I do odd jobs for them around the garage and garden. The first time I walk into their house, Lois sits at the piano, a black baby grand which hunkers before a window looking out across the valley and the distant mountains. She seems to partake of the mountain herself, firmly perched there, formal, implacable. She is blond, rather feline, self-contained, with a placidity that suggests a lake surface shimmering over incalculable depths; like her husband, she's only partially knowable. She is a soprano who performs with local choirs, in musicals Shirley has directed, in an opera troupe—and today she is singing Kurt Weill, "Pirate Jenny," from *The Threepenny Opera*, in German. The chords are heavy, mordant; her voice is sonorous and chill at once, full of history and resonance. I'm supposed to be fetching a bucket or something, but I don't move. I stand transfixed, imagining what it would be like to have these people for parents, suddenly full of envy for their son, feeling I've been permitted entrance to a life so far from anything I've known. Then Lois notices me, but she doesn't stop playing, she simply looks right at me, acknowledging my presence as her listener, though her face seems entirely filled by the music, haunted by it, as she sings, "And the ship, the black freighter, turns round out to sea . . . ."

∽

I've a survivor's resources; I've sharpened my senses. I can sniff the wind; I can feel when the storms are brewing in the house. When my mother's on the rampage I can find a place to sleep, get myself fed, and better: find some good company, some ways to play, some people who want to read my poems or paint with me or just hang out in the park.

I have even discovered a method of achieving moments of tranquillity, courtesy of Dino. If he has not given up his elaborate hash pipe, he's at least set it down long enough to pursue a new interest, Transcendental Meditation. He's been initiated over the summer, while he's been away somewhere, and returned with a zeal for conversion. I am the perfect subject for proselytizing; the technique promises expanded consciousness and creativity, and ultimately release from the karmic wheel of constant reincarnation, as well as a natural high. I don't have the money to join up, but Dino intervenes with some family resources, and soon I'm waiting in his living room with the required devotional objects: a clean handkerchief, a flower, and a piece of fruit. I'm led into a darkened room where a visiting meditation teacher—a black-bearded professor on leave from UCLA—tells me my new mantra, a one-syllable Sanskrit word that sends me off promptly into gales of laughter that seem to come from nowhere. "You're releasing stress," I'm told, and indeed I love floating off on the mantra's sonic pillow, an experience not unlike my out-of-the-body traveling: let go, let go further—a deeper and deeper trance that sometimes leads me to states of mind where I can see my thoughts billow up out of silence like balloons, or see the colors of the birdsong I'm hearing out the window: shades of surrealism.

Neither Dino or I are quite willing to give up getting stoned, so we alternate Dionysian weekends with weekdays of spiritual practice, except when we travel off to a meditation retreat in the mountains outside of town. There we meditate all day long, in adjacent rooms of the retreat house, getting driftier and driftier, and in the evening all the meditators gather to listen to the Maharishi lecturing on tape: "Consciousness," he intones in an odd high voice, each syllable deliberate, chiming, a little pinched, "is a lake. Sink down into the lake, put down your roots like the lotus." The guru's metaphoric universe is exotic and highly limited: everything's mountain, lotus, root.

∽

My style's a kind of resourcefulness, too. My hippie clothes—getting more raggedy, since home gets stranger, and my parents have forgotten about shopping, and do I really want things that speak of their world anyway, like underwear? I love the colors of the weird and beautiful outfits the Hog Farmers wear, citizens of a New Mexican commune who've come to town on their magic bus, and parked the painted extravaganza in the middle of the Yippie Free Festival, where Dino and I have danced all afternoon, each of us high on a package of Romilar, an over-the-counter antihistamine that makes you fly, if you take enough of it. Today the music carries me up and up, and when the crowd applauds the clapping enters my forehead like a thousand shining little needles. I'm so high I don't notice when somebody steals my new shoes, handmade leather moccasins that don't have soles but sort of wrap around your feet so you can feel the earth. They cinch at the top with a loop of leather that threads through two brass circles, but now I'll never loop them again. Oh, well—somebody needed those shoes more than I did.

My friend Anna's at every free festival, immensely pregnant, radiant; her boyfriend's an acid dealer I know, a dark-skinned Hispanic boy with plum-colored lips and long eyelashes. Anna knows her baby's going to be beautiful. The boyfriend picks up whole suitcases full of LSD at the airport; he has to wear gloves to count it because the stuff's so strong he'll get high just from the residue penetrating the skin of his fingers. I know it's true because I bought some from him once, an envelope of white powder, and after I licked my finger walked into a Baskin-Robbins: not thirty-one flavors but thirty-one hundred heavens of color, a tantric paradise glowing like the keyboard chords in the Donovan song, in those saturated hues: Havana Lake, Rose Carmethine. Anna's a little worried because she's tripped once while she was pregnant, but in her heart she feels the baby's okay.

And he is; next time I see her there's Alexander Moonbow, right against her breast, his little fingers reaching for my patchy new beard, his own luscious black hair curling. "We live out in the desert now," Anna says. "In a trailer. Just me and little Moonshine. It's lonely, but you ought to see the stars."

In a downtown park, over which looms a big can of paint, a billboard that glowers like a huge Pop icon, my friend Janey (another misfit from drama class) and I sit on a bench. She's in her minidress and Power to the People button; I'm in my usual array of layers and jewels; I have a kind of John Lennon look (from the *Two Virgins* period) going: tangly long hair cascading down my back, a scraggly beard. It's sundown, silence all around us except for the pigeons, and she pulls from her purse a little brass walnut, hinged. Somehow that little thing seems to me now the icon of the times: a little world springs open, and gives you what? A treasure, freedom, boundlessness, which in this instance turns out to be two hits of the nastiest acid I'll ever encounter, chocolate chip, a guaranteed eight hours of paranoia and despair. We have an awful evening, lonely, even though we're together, horribly confused, afraid of our shadows, afraid of each other's voices, sure that everything is a lie. We sit in a black-light pizza parlor on Speedway and watch each other's teeth glow while some guy tells us stories that don't make any sense, involving us in the thread of a tale and then dropping it and telling us we've imagined it all. What "it"? What "all"? We wind up in a Fourth Avenue dive pouring sugar into cups of orange juice because we've heard that niacinamide and sugar will cut a bad trip short, but we just sit there being miserable for hours, the fluorescent lights bouncing off our eyeballs, the fillings in my teeth radiating, I'm convinced, the black light I've absorbed. I'm frying from the inside out.

A better trip occurs on my day with Patsy Pelmet, whose name is so funny that she's always called by the entire thing. Patsy's a big strapping girl with clouds of frizzy pinkish hair—a white girl's 'fro—and beautiful flocks of freckles. She's wearing jeans and an embroidered Mexican top. We drop mescaline in the park before noon, and do what all day? Lie on the grass and watch clouds, swing on the swings a little, involve ourselves in the slow activities of the grass, groove on the water in the fountain, get seriously sun-burned, sing: "Wear your love like heaven," conjuring the colors in the lyrics, Prussian Blue, Alizarin Crimson—colors of the oil tubes in my mother's abandoned paint box. Her last painting: a bowl of lilacs, the dab of paint delineating each petal thicker than the last, the whole thing shadowy, wet looking, smoldering. In the room where she used to paint—Orlin's old room—the drawers clink when you open them, heavy with empty bottles, hollow cargo.

Coming down, Patsy and I walk to my house. It's late, my parents are in bed. We build a fire in the fireplace and watch, the last of the drug still enchanting everything, the lick and dazzle of flames liquid, arching into air like the individual blades of grass in the park. It's very romantic, the fire, the darkened room, and Patsy would like to ball; that's how she puts it: "Come on, man, let's ball." I like the feeling of kissing her, rubbing up against each other, the pour of awareness the aftereffect of the drug makes, this timelessness, I could almost . . .

Almost. I pull back, I say, "My parents are in their room, I don't know . . . ." I say, "Must be the dope, I'm pretty fried." And she says, "Yeah, I'm pretty fried too," and pulls her pants back up where she'd loosened them.

11

Sorrowful Mother

My mother taught me to love the things that would save me, and then, when I was sixteen, she taught me that I wasn't worth saving. I learned the first lesson best—since beauty engaged my deepest interest, and since I was most willing to be instructed by delight—but I would be lying if I said that the second lesson didn't shape me.

When I was a boy, in the years of our art lessons, she allowed me to paint a still life with her oils on a piece of Masonite, a green pottery bowl full of feathery orange chrysanthemums I invented stroke by swirly stroke. She bent over my shoulder, saying something like, *Look how that blue you've added makes the bowl curve toward you, look how it makes the green deepen and come alive.* There we are together, permanent in my memory as pigment suspended in oil, the unmistakable tenderness of her gesture, her shoulder barely touching mine, as we both turn our attention toward something we can love.

Is the nature of the instruction we receive from our parents always contradictory, despite their best intentions? My mother seemed to hold out the world with one hand and sought to diminish me with the other, as if to say, *Here, love, is a paradise you do not merit.*

∾

The book I buy at Star Drug is a paperback called *That Special Summer*. I like to go there after school for a Coke and french fries, delaying the return home, and peruse the rack of books in the front of the store. This one sings to me; doesn't that man on the cover, darkly blond, with green eyes of a striking immediacy, seem to be looking right at me? His gaze guarantees that the $1.95 paperbacks cast onto the waters of American drugstores will find their way surely (like Baby Moses in the bulrushes) to the places where they are desired.

The book is basically pornography, though it involves a plot, in which a reluctant older man is seduced by a teenager, the son of the older man's heterosexual friend. What matters to me isn't the story but the absolute raging heat of the sex scenes, which are detailed, nearly constant, and so hot as to make the book threaten to wrinkle and ignite in my hands. I devour it; I devour it again; I can't stop. Here is one sentence I remember to this day: "His nipples were pink and promising as surprise packages." (A memory that makes me glad I no longer own the book, and so can't tarnish the memory of its intensity through a reencounter with its prose style.)

Having lived in it, having carried it around secretly, reread the best parts, exhausted it (and myself) for the time being, I face the problem of what to do with it. I feel I should hide it, of course, but hiding actually makes matters worse, potentially, especially since Alicia comes to clean once a week, and though I complain that I can't find anything after she comes, that she disturbs my papers and books, it's to no avail. I could throw the book away, but I can't bear to part with it. I can't ask anyone to keep it for me. So I think the thing to do is to be nonchalant about it, to act as if it is just like any other book, a story bearing no particular resemblance to the circumstances of my life. I put it on my bookshelf, in a calculatedly unplaced way. Why should anyone bother to notice *That Special Summer*?

So when it's gone one day, when I look everywhere, quietly frantic, and then discover it's on the bookcase in my parents' room, I don't say anything. I don't move it, since any gesture to call attention to it would make things worse. "Oh," I plan to say, "it's just a book I found someplace, something I picked up. Different, huh?" I leave it beside books of my mother's, *Gone With the Wind* and a paperback novel called *Mandingo*, its cover decked with a sweaty giant of a black man stripped to the waist, chains around his wrists, his face a mask of lust, while a startlingly white woman, nightgown nearly as pale as her skin, swoons at his feet. My mother had thought it disgusting, and read it straight through.

One day she's drunk, that scowl on her face that means: *Stay clear*. I try to just go on about my business like everything's fine, but she says, "How would you like a stick up your ass?"

I say I don't know what she's talking about, and she says that's what men do to each other, her face twisted into a mask of revulsion. She's swaying a little, a fierce hen, confrontational.

I am unbelievably embarrassed and uncomfortable. But somehow I get this courage—because she's drunk?—and before I think what I'm saying, I argue, "Well, is that so different from what a man and a woman do?"

Pause. She says, "No, no it's not." She's quiet for a minute and then she says, "The woman's part is no good." A thought which takes her out of my affairs and into the familiar twilight of her own weeping; she stumbles to her room, as if all her anger's dissolved now, something dark washed over her. It's like the opening image of a soap opera she used to watch, *The Edge of Night*; each weekday noon it would be daylight in the city, the skyline clear, and then a diagonal of shadow would fall across the buildings, the trees, the sky itself, while the announcer said, "*The* Edge *of Night*." That visible borderline would hang there, transparent but still dark, permanent, shadowing half the world.

∽

Now it's really night. Where have I been? Out to Dino's, listening to rock 'n' roll, burning incense to cover the smell of our joint; I know better than to bring anyone to my house now, haven't for years. Or maybe I've been to the park, lying out on the grass on my back to look at the stars, making them leave light trails behind them by moving my head back and forth, as if I'm drawing on the sky with my own eyeballs. Or out to a group meditation at the university, everyone soaking up the collective tranquillity generated by all that transcendence? Or was it the bad trip, the night I thought my bones were smoldering? I was about to burst into flame from the inside out, and only my will could control it, or keep it almost in check. Then I was that boy I'd been the terrible night of the haircut: *hide him, nobody wants to look at him.*

Maybe I've been to the music store where I sleep some nights; it belongs to the uncle of a friend—Ray, my latest crush, another unavailable straight boy; is there any other kind out there? His parents are likewise unpredictable, so it gives us both a place to go, stretching out blankets on the floor between the racks of sheet music and the guitars and drum sets that gleam in the neon glow from the front window. Ray sits up in his underpants, all milk and blue-veined shadow, strumming on his guitar the songs he writes; I smoke and listen admiringly. Ray's in love with Diane, Diane's in love with me; together we all sit by her parents' pool, on mescaline, and turn her mother's collection of art-glass paperweights in our hands, right in front of our eyes: cities of light, seen from high above the earth. It's the pattern of my teenage nights: my father slips me ten bucks, twenty bucks, says quietly, "Get lost," and I do. Twenty bucks is a treasure: dinner at the pancake house, a pack of Camels, bottle of patchouli oil, take a friend to the movies, the all-night coffee shop: there, that's used hours and hours of the night, which smells, in Tucson, like oleanders, like cooled dust, somebody's sprinkler running on a midnight lawn. Three A.M., four?

Into the house quietly; it's the way to come back home, tentatively, days after the last big scene, see if you can just sort of appear, probably no one will say anything. They never lock the kitchen door, and it's strange to step into the house, after the freshness and immensity of the night, which is so unwearied and promising. The swamp-box cooler chills the room; the atmosphere of the house is turbulent and static at once, as if you could see the grief in the air, as if the whole place were blurry with the smear of somebody's anger. The heavy pendulum of the clock swings out its assigned arc, sounds like its name: *clock*-swing, *clock*-swing. Quiet now, past the cabinets scrolled with their curlicues and flowers. Around the corner, down the hall, but they aren't asleep, or she's not. She's talking, as if she's been talking all night to him, to the wall, re-counting her litany of grief, telling the beads of her sorrows, voice you've heard through the walls for years, sour voice seeping into the adobe walls like some oily pigment, this rag of a house soaking it in till its ready to combust. This time you hear her plain: "Son's a homosexual and Sally's a whore." But you go on past their door, into your room, the lights are out, and you're hoping you're not visible at all, not even a shadow. You close your door as slowly as you can, so that the hinges will make no noise, and you can sleep now, in your own bed, and though she hasn't stopped saying things you can't make out now through the wall between you, you're tired enough to sleep regardless.

∽

I have a little shrine I brought home from San Francisco, an up-right wooden box painted celestial blue, with a yellow horse floating on a field of stars. The wooden door slides open, so that the box becomes a little theater, revealing its interior. It used to hold three crude images of gods—Brahma, Vishnu, Shiva—but they didn't speak to me, so I've replaced them with one perfect smooth river stone I found someplace, a token of—fixity, I think, serenity.

Which I reach for also with the Nepalese rope incense I burn in my room, with albums of the smoky and swirling music of the sitar, Ravi Shankar playing evening ragas, with the mantra that steadies and calms as it sinks down toward silence, like my stone thrown into a deep lake. Soothing, elemental vocabulary of the Maharishi: *stone, water, lake.*

The vocabulary of my poems is elemental, too, but not espe-cially soothing. More hallucinatory, narcotic; from the poets I've been reading I've learned to employ images in my poems, objects which serve as vessels of feeling I couldn't name. They recur from poem to poem, diamonds and thunderclouds, pearls and chande-liers, maps and smoke. They aren't good poems, far from it, but they betray a certain precocious intoxication with language, an enchantment with style—or at least an ability to learn the style of the hour, and copy it fiercely. And there's something more here, too, perhaps: evidence of an inner life, the uncharted landscape of *within*, which seems as various as the desert, its night equally blue and fragrant, awash with stars.

A poet whose work I've read comes to my creative writing class at Rincon; it seems a minor miracle, that Charles Simic should be sitting there, in our basement room, on a plain Tuesday morning. I own his book *Dismantling the Silence*, and I love both the collage on the cover (blood vessels conjoined, in a surrealist marriage, to the parts of a machine) and the cool and dreamy poems within: Simic goes inside a stone and reads the star charts on the inner walls; he listens to what the grass says, he takes apart silence as though it were a huge piece of furniture.

And now here he is, the dreamer in the flesh. He's in town to give a reading at the university, and Dick Shelton has made sure he's come to visit here. My teacher says, "Mark, would you read Mr. Simic one of your poems?"

I do. He leans back in his chair, appraising, eyes on me; he listens intently, taking every phrase in. There's a pause, when I'm done, which seems to me quite a long one. And then he leans forward, nodding, his round little glasses glinting in the light. In his lush eastern European accent he says, "Read me another one," which is the very best thing he could say, the perfect thing.

∾

I've come from school, she's in her room with that drunk, lost look on her face; it's an ordinary day. She actually seems to shrink when she drinks, as if her being were all concentrated in her face, and the effort of all that intensity somehow diminished the rest of her.

I've gone to my room to put away my books, my notebook covered with inked peace signs and slogans, the denim jacket whose back I've embroidered in swirls of silky floss. Then she calls me out into the hall. She says, *Son, come on out here.*

And I do. She's standing at the other end of the hallway, by the doorway to the kitchen, holding the black pistol in both hands, my father's Luger, holding it the way he taught her to years ago, when we used to shoot at bottles and cans in the desert: well out in front of her, away from her face.

She holds the gun out, and she waits; I stand in the line of fire, and I wait.

And now we're in a movie: oh God, a safety movie. I can only see us—them—through a diminishing lens, the telescope's wrong end: they're tiny, in the impossibly elongated hall, the mother swaying a little from side to side in order to maintain her balance, her eye lined up with the sight at the top of the pistol, lined up with the heart of the boy, who stands with his hands at his side, as if in acquiescence. They've been moving toward this moment for years, mother and son, and now they don't move at all, except for her slight swaying.

What I don't know is: does she pull the trigger?

Does she hesitate, does her hand refuse the task she's set it? I want her to hesitate, but perhaps she merely goes ahead and squeezes, maybe again and again, I don't know. I don't know because I'm not there. I'm closed, gone away, already dead behind the eyes, no longer at home, halfway to the next life already and good riddance to this one. Where is it we go, when we leave the body? Maybe I'm thinking I won't miss it, this sorry stubborn queer flesh, maybe I'm thinking nothing at all, merely empty, ready to receive what my mother offers.

Firebird

That hallway opens on and on, in the nightmare house of the perspective box, a narrow gullet of space telescoping further and further, boy at one end, mother at the other, the bullet—fired or unfired, does it matter?—traversing that length, never arriving, since time dilates there, too, the hallway traveling on for years, the uncertain duration of a lifetime.

∾

They are the twin poles of an education, these two images, the terms which establish the parameters of my life. A boy lifted by music, his body become aerial and bright as the phoenix that music portrays—and that boy, years later, turning to ash, held in the sights of his mother's gun. The gun his father's taught her to use, the father who'll come home in a while and find them standing there, and find that his wife hasn't killed his son because she can't get the safety off.

Of course it matters, that the bullet wasn't fired. I lived. I wanted to live, or at least, now, in the reinvention of the past that remembering is, I want to; I don't want to miss my life, I don't want to miss anything.

And yet, once attempted, the act of obliteration isn't erasable. To raise a gun and aim is to will a death, and that act of will is ineradicable; it is that moment of willed darkness that is still traveling down the hallway toward me, and though the tunnel stretches on and on, though I run ahead, am propelled forward in time away from the bullet and its fierce momentum, that gesture never ends. From that moment on I am a boy whose mother wanted him to die (but, oh, I was that before, wasn't I?) and I hurry, running ahead of her wish.

Just as that hallway narrows on and on, the familiar limits of space dilated, the trustworthy nature of rooms and houses violated, so that any familiar space might suddenly open out, endlessly—just so, time begins to move differently, too, now, in this story. A life hurtles forward, tumbles out and ahead from these twin poles: firebird and revolver, diametrical opposites like the yes and no which rule the Ouija board: twin magnetic poles which cause a kind of gyroscopic spin, advancing the motion of my tale.

Much remains in the margin, of course, much at the edges that isn't part of this narrative. Having pulled back the curtains on a source of light and an equally potent wellspring of darkness, what more could I say, to tell you how I began?

I could tell you we won't say a word about what's happened, not a single word. The gun goes back in its drawer, my father sits with my mother on the couch and gets up to bring her a drink while she reviles me, and him; he rubs her feet when she cries because her back aches. I go to school, go out, go anywhere. I get along, get by, get numb, and it won't be long before I hurry away from high school and them. I'll try running away—as I did once to San Francisco, I'll flee now to Seattle and to Vancouver, to a nameless hotel, $3.50 a night, with a big red neon sign outside my window that hangs the vertical red word RESIDENTIAL above the street, which seems always wet with rain. From my window the harbor shimmers all night, just beyond the rooftops across the street, and I sit in the window frame atop the chilly silver of the radiator and watch the tankers and the cargo ships, trying to imagine what's next. But I'm not ready, don't know what to do; it's my father's steady supply of tens and twenties that's sheltered me, a safety net that kept me from living on the streets. I'd come close enough to it, those years, to know what that was like, to know a longhaired kid without a dollar to his name didn't have a place to turn to.

So I go back home and sign myself up at the university. I don't tell them I haven't finished high school and, weirdly, they don't ask. It's a big state school, and they're easy, and by the time they find out it's a moot point anyway. I find friends in the poetry work shop, and in the loose coalition of hippies and politicos and lost souls who are my peers, in 1970, the great loose flow of us marching downtown to the draft board to end the war, nonviolent principles dissolving as we smash into the army recruiting center and tear it apart: cardboard figures of soldiers, men and women, thrown over our heads, trampled to pieces.

But the train that takes me away from home, finally, is the same train my mother and sister leapt onto: I enter into a wildly mistaken marriage—too young (I am seventeen), too confused (if I act straight will I be straight?)—and somehow wily nonetheless: love's a means of travel, a window into another life, a world apart from the one I've known. If I'm lying to myself, then it's also true that I'm making my way forward; if I'm living with someone I can't wholly commit to, then at least she isn't trying to kill me.

I don't really plan to get married; Ruth and I start living together, in an old white Spanish-style apartment building in a beat-up neighborhood between school and downtown, across the street from a mortuary where bats fly out of the eaves every night and circle above the street lamps and the blooming oleanders. She's a graduate student, a poet who composes her work in a mild state of trance, to my mind enchantingly eccentric, given to big hats and grand gestures and apparently completely oblivious to the fact that she's old enough to be my mother. One day she says her friends want to know when we're getting married. I say, "October?"

Of course I can't see that I'm being deeply loyal to my parents. I've married a woman who sees herself as a misunderstood artist, too sensitive and interior for this world; I somehow don't notice how drunk she gets at parties, how her face crumples and shifts when she drinks; it's only on weekends, only every once in a while. I can't see that I'm doing just what my father did, signing on to take care of a woman who refuses responsibility for herself. I'm doing just what I felt I should do as a boy: rescue that woman, make her happy, be the one who will please her, at any cost. Years later I'll shudder and laugh at once in my shrink's office, when we talk about the fact that my mother and my ex-wife have the same first name: two Ruths, two strange fusions of Southern-lady vulnerability and wills of steel. I don't know any of that now. At seventeen I'm barely learning to live outside my parents' house. You could say I am hiding from myself, which I am, or running away from home, which is also true. But at least I am stumbling toward safety; I'm lost, and any strong pole, any anchor will do. I am fumbling my way through the unchartable territory of sex, of my first foolish tries at adult love, though the notion of a life founded in my own desire is still a prospect unimaginably far away.

∽

I'll live far away from my mother, while she's drinking herself to death in my old olive-and-adobe bedroom, those desert colors I chose years ago. We'll talk on the phone, Saturdays, and over the five more years she'll live I'll hear that voice go from querulous and difficult and somehow glad to hear from me all at once to something vaguer, more diffuse, finally merely a ramble and drift and disconnection. She sees ghosts in her bedroom; she dreams her dead brother comes and brushes out her hair. Later I'll find out her brother isn't dead—but he is, of course, to her: she is at such a huge distance from the past, she has traveled to some isolation where no one can follow, and the vodka (does she still even need to drink?) and tranquilizers and God knows what else seal off her room, consign her to darkness and murmurs and then silence.

∽

"Your father," my mother says, trying to sit up in the hospital bed, raising her head to look me directly in the eye, urgent, confiding, "has nailed my hands to these boards."

Why tell a story like this, who wants to read it?

A writer I know says, *Say it clearly and you make it beautiful, no matter what.* Sometimes I think that's true; difficult experience can be redeemed by the powers of language, and words can help us to see what is graceful or human where loveliness and humanity seem to fail.

But other days I believe it's the other way round: say it beautifully, or at least precisely, say it as exactly as you can, and you will make it clear. Clarity isn't in the service of beauty; it's the other way around. The older I get, the more I distrust redemption; it isn't in the power of language to repair the damages. Here is a sentence which cannot be redeemed: "Your father has nailed my hands to these boards."

What we remember, wrote the poet who was my first teacher of the art, *can be changed. What we forget we are always.* Dick was right: We live the stories we tell; the stories we don't tell live us. What you don't allow yourself to know controls and determines; whatever's held to the light "can be changed"—not the facts, of course, but how we understand them, how we live with them. Everyone will be filled by grief, distorted by sorrow; that's the nature of being a daughter or a son, as our parents are also. What matters is what we learn to make of what happens to us.

And we learn to make, I think, by telling. Held to the light of common scrutiny, nothing's ever quite as unique as our shame and sorrow would have us think. But if you don't say it, you're alone with it, and the singularity of your story seems immense, intractable. And isn't that part of what brought her to this bed, to these nailed wrists, in the first place: her isolation?

Even sad stories are company. And perhaps that's why you might read such a chronicle, to look into a companionable darkness that isn't yours. Proximity is the best consolation; place the griefs beside one another and watch them diminish. We seem to need to hear, Yes, I've known something like that, too.

But the story lives in the details, those sharp bits of experience to which emotion is attached, the way kelp and sea wrack cling to bits of stone and shell. Hell is in the details: I haven't said it clearly, the terror of it, the diminishment, the horror and pity, the selfish fear and pity for myself even in the face of her pain, how I want to draw close to her and also don't think I can stand to look, want to help and am entirely helpless.

Try again: "Your father," my mother says, "has nailed my hands to these boards." She tries to sit up in the hospital bed, but manages only to raise her head so she can look me directly in the eye, conspiratorial, desperate. Her room is high in Tucson's University Hospital, the unmistakable profile of those mountains out the window, a dozen shades of smoke blue. Her hands *are* attached to boards because she is being fed intravenously, and in her delirium she thrashes so that the tubes are pulled from her wrists, or else she tries to yank them out, so they've been secured by white elastic tape that holds the plastic and bandages in place. She lifts them in the air, miserably, toward me; she wants me to see what has been done to her, as if now that I have come surely I will understand her, I of all people will believe her when she tells how he's tortured her, and how the orderlies come in the night to rape her—she says, come with hooks and with pepper and an arsenal of poisons that burn and sting.

Oh, God, I think, I can't look.

I'm twenty-three, living halfway across the country, and my father's called and said, "If you ever want to see your mother alive again, you'd better come now." He's given me the money to fly back home.

But he hasn't told me how she'll look, dying of cirrhosis of the liver. Just like the last time he brought me to see her in a hospital room, after I'd moved out of the house and gone to live in the Geronimo Hotel, a faded adobe-colored wreck of a place near the university, where you could pay your rent by the week. He'd said, "Your mother wants to see you," and picked me up in front of the stuccoed courtyard with its sad grass. But then he'd driven in silence past the turn for the house, driven without a word but "You'll see where we're going" right to the hospital parking lot, and never told me how she'd dropped a cigarette lighter onto her nightgown and covered her breasts with third-degree burns; "I got what I deserved," she said as soon as she saw me, "to be burned at the stake."

(Do you tell the story out of horror, a kind of purgation? Out of an old but abiding rage, because part of you wants to get even? Or because it's your single truest possession: what do you own as much as you do what frightens you most? Maybe it's simple: you tell the story to find out why you have to tell it.)

My father lets me find things out for myself, so he hasn't said she's jaundiced now, her skin an evil yellow; hasn't said her long hair's falling out, every day, when he comes to the hospital and sits beside her and brushes it. He hasn't said that her stomach's enormous, as if she's hugely pregnant, since her poisoned liver's given up and swollen her abdomen with the toxins it will not admit.

There is so much he has not told me: how he'd decided to let her die at home, after this last year she's spent in bed or in a wheelchair, obliterated on vodka and prescription tranquilizers. Where have they come from, these boxes of Miltown? Was he just going to keep her as quiet as he could, keep her from living in pain, and wait it out? Maybe he thought, How could she want anything else now, but to die? What else has she wanted for years? And so was he being perversely, brutally kind, bringing her the pills and the vodka? But then she got so sick, he couldn't bear it, even he had to fold and put her in someone else's hands. "I've never seen anyone," her doctor said to me, "brought to the hospital in such an advanced state of deterioration."

Maybe he thought if he gave her the pills she wouldn't drink, wouldn't be driven by her furies to lash at him and at herself. Maybe if he kept her still she'd live.

She seems to think he's murdering her, but she's mad, isn't she, this woman I recognize and don't? What can I do but look, while my father's left us alone, gone off to the cafeteria for lunch, outside for a walk? He must be numb with it, he must be nearly mad himself with grief; he's inert, passive, a cork floating on water so much larger than him, its direction nothing to do with his choosing. He fills me with such a combination of rage and sadness that I can hardly talk. I want to get away from him, I want to drive around alone in his car and look at the desert, at the town I've left, I want to touch a stranger till I am senseless with it, I want to get lost. What comes out of me are tears, then silence, then nothing. We are null and blank when we're together, he and I, though he is also seething. We go to the Red Lobster for a seafood dinner. When the waiter says, "Are you finished, sir?" a little too soon, he says, "If you touch my plate I'll stick this fork in your hand."

She also thinks everybody wants to hurt her; every man wants to—I've never before heard her say it—fuck her, penetrate or violate the ruin of her. Every man but me. I discover I can not only look at her but talk to her, and she to me, and though she thrashes when she talks about my father and the conspiracies against her, there are little openings, moments when something crosses her mind that seems to calm her, if only for a second. Soon I find that if I can keep her attention fixed on these topics, her body will relax a bit, grow still.

The subjects which soothe her most are African violets, dogs, and Mexico. When we talk about these things I take the brush and brush her hair slowly, a stroking which also seems to steady her. I am good with the mad, at home out here on the edge of the world where the dying are, and I come closer to her as she is falling apart under my gaze, her hair coming loose even with the easy strokes of the brush. She begins a story which combines the elements that please her. She has bought a house in Mexico, just across the border, she says, in the hills above Nogales. She has told no one, and I must not tell anyone either, especially my father, who would prevent her from going. She will live there with her friend Alicia, who used to come once a week to scrub and dust; I don't know how long it's been since my mother's seen Alicia, but everything has been planned: they will be happy in the new house, which will have a courtyard, and a garden, and in the kitchen with its blue-and-white tiled counters they will raise African violets, white ones. They will have a perfect dog, a German shepherd, devoted to them both, who will walk with them down the steep hill into the village, those occasional days when they must go to town. She would like me to bring her a white violet, and a book about dogs. She must prepare.

In truth I don't look for these things; I think she won't remember, and I am mad myself, that night, lurching, lost, driving around, terrified, coming back to sleep in the stillness and heaviness of my parents' house, the swamp cooler on the roof humming over the darkened rooms, the familiar displays of my mother's blue-and-white china—chipped, crazed stuff—dusty now, smudged with smoke and cobwebs. After she dies my father won't let Alicia in the house because she might move something, put a platter or a pitcher back in the wrong place; every gesture my mother made, every arrangement of her collection, will seem to him precious. Outside in the dark, sleepless, I study the new houses crawling up the sides of the foothills, a brilliant scatter of mica chips, also blue and white, with little glimmers of amber. Behind me, in the house, scattered evidence of my mother's illness: bedpan, oxygen tank, boxes and boxes of Miltown.

The next morning, sunlight on the mountains, the sky scrubbed pale, heat wavering up off the hospital parking lot. My mother says, "Did you bring me a white violet and the book about dogs?" I'd been sure she'd forget. I confess I haven't. "That's all right," she says, the last thing she'll ever say to me. "It's funny how so many things just don't make a difference."

Standing by the open casket, in the funeral home in Tucson, I find myself suddenly lashing out at my family, at my father and my sister. "You didn't understand her like I did," I practically shout at them. "Nobody understood her like I did; you don't understand, she was mine."

They look at me bewildered; I'm addled by loss, senseless, I can't explain. We follow the hearse from the church—someplace in the foothills I've never been—out to a vast expanse of desert which has been bulldozed and irrigated into a thankless stretch of grass. No markers are allowed to rise above the ground, so that the grim turf may be easily mowed; each grave gets a little plastic-covered metal plaque, the name on paper beneath it. Will my father replace this with a flat stone bearing her name? I don't know. I have never been there again.

My sister married the man she met in the bar by the air base, had a child, and before long they moved from Tucson, off to Reno, where he found a job in gambling, working as the "pit boss" on one floor of a large casino, where he supervised racks and racks of jingling slot machines, and the sly green blackjack tables and rattling roulette wheels. She's worked in casinos, too, hostessing in their big, heavily air-conditioned restaurants. She's with him still, to this day. We talk on the phone, holidays, but we don't talk about our parents all that much; it makes us both too nervous. Sally's youngest daughter's in college now. The children she lost at the end of that first juvenile marriage have come to live in the desert near her. They have children of their own, who splash every weekend in their grandmother's swimming pool, from which they can hear the steady roar of the new freeway that's barreled through their neighborhood, just a few streets away.

∿

My father's pistol reverberated longer because it wasn't fired, ringing into my future, and into his.

But my other token of the past had a future, too.

The Firebird, in fact, is used to the gun, and doesn't care about the difficulty of circumstance; if anything, it burns brighter in a gloomy wood. *Go ahead*, the blazing thing says, *do what you will, I'll find the music in it.*

Show me what I can't use.

∿

I believe that art saved my life. How is it that making sustains?

I had these examples, this gift, given by my mother, by Miss Tynes in our fourth-grade classroom full of our drawings and plaster sculptures, our paintings and stitcheries. By Stravinsky, by the hands of the old masters translated into light projected on the walls of our house in Tucson so many years ago. By Little Miss Sunbeam, that polished prodigy; by Judy Garland's visibly broken heart, the microphone cord tossed over her narrow shoulder as if she could do anything casually; by Miss Stephanie; by the loony old man building his grottoes of broken glass and pottery shards in the Valley of the Moon. By Dick Shelton, and Lois thundering at the piano, by Charlie Simic pushing back his glasses and eyeing me like a Slavic owl.

The gift was a faith in the life of art, or, more precisely, a sense that there was a life which was not mine, but to which I was welcome to join myself. A life which was larger than any single person's, and thus not one to be claimed, but to apprentice oneself to. In the larger, permanent community of makers, you could be someone by being no one, by disappearing into what you made. In that life your hands were turned, temporarily, to what beauty wanted, what spirit—not your spirit, not exactly—desired: to come into being, to be seen.

No matter what else, I worked, and worked feverishly: late nights at a succession of instruments which show, like calendar pages falling in an old movie, the progression of time: the Smith-Corona manual, the electric portable, the secondhand self-correcting IBM (so dear and long coveted!), the Brother with the daisy-wheel that remembered a whole line of type at a time. I wrote endlessly, poems and stories and even a hopeless and hallucinatory novel. Because I was in hiding from myself, because so little of my life had entered the realm of the sayable, my writing was inchoate, veiled. But it was charged with feeling—rage and longing, mostly, though I couldn't read that then. I practiced my neosurrealism, a perfect disguise for the heart. Reams of paper, boxes and baskets of old manuscripts, half of them squirreled away somewhere still. It wasn't wasted effort; I was at least playing my scales, investing, in some way, in what might be. And I was honoring my mother, fulfilling one of her wishes for me, not the wish that I'd die but the hope that I'd thrive.

A neighbor boy told me once, delivering the paper, how after midnight he'd hear the clacking hurry of my typewriter drifting from my attic study to his room. He liked it, he said, the late, lonely sound of someone working.

∾

It took me nine years to leave my marriage, to kick and struggle my way out. Just as I moved into my new apartment, the first place I'd ever lived alone, my father remarried. A strange moment: there we were, sitting in my shabby student apartment in Des Moines, the contrast between us unspoken and plain: I'd left a woman I couldn't save, only gradually coming to understand that it was arrogance and vanity to think I might help her. And my father, of course, had remained loyal; he'd never freed himself from his drunken wife, and it was years after her death before he married again.

We sat at the round table I'd covered with a white sheet, Larry and Edith and I, in the newly painted white dining room, and we drank the beer my father had brought. We were all guarded at first, but the beer made the conversation loosen. He seemed unsettled, annoyed by the distance between us, baffled by my divorce. He said, "Remember when your mother tried to shoot you with that gun?"

Sudden clamor in my head, sudden pulse-stop. The fact is I can't remember, not even a fraction of the scene, a flash of detail, though I know it happened, can feel myself start to sweat the second he mentions it, feel the dizzy gravity of it, but I don't remember it at all. I've locked it away in a concrete bunker, buried it down in the dark.

"I had to sell that gun after that," he says. "I always liked that gun."

I have wished to see this man roundly, not to turn him into a shadow or an easily explained cartoon. I would like to be above loathing my father, and I want to believe that we cannot hate what we really know. But I can't accept this; I can't bear the idea that he prefers his gun, that what was lost, in that moment was his beloved weapon; isn't it time, now, for an apology, a gesture of regret, a . . . what? What could set this right between us?

There's no getting around it: I hate him for this.

Twenty years after we buried my mother in that resentful, unvisited turf, my father reads a book I've written. It's a memoir about grief, the bitter wake of my lover's death, and in it I have described the urge to take my own life, in a hopeless hour when I didn't believe I could find the strength to participate in the world again, when pleasure seemed to lead only toward endings.

Of course I didn't write the book thinking I was speaking to my father. If I thought he'd be listening, I'm not at all sure what I could have said. But that's a miracle of the page; it feels private, interior, an intimate chamber, but it's an intimacy with all the doors and windows open.

I described walking the salt marshes in winter, at the end of Cape Cod, how their austerity and immensity suited my own grief. My father, at eighty-three, writes me a letter. He describes the way he'd walk the swampy edges of the Mississippi himself, sixty years ago, and how he loved the red-winged blackbirds that darted there, and the huge owl who'd turn his head to watch my father pass, and how in spring floods the farmers' fields would sometimes fill with fish. He remembered a toothless bulldog he used to feed boiled hominy. My father is a master of non sequitur—he once wrote me a letter which passed from his approval of my divorce to the number of watermelons ripening in his garden within a single sentence—and so I wasn't surprised that his letter suddenly shifted registers. What startled me was what he said: how he understood, reading my book, how I'd felt when I wanted to jump from a hotel balcony. He told me a story, how he'd been so discouraged, in 1975, that he'd emptied his bank account, took his pistol, parked the county truck he drove in a garage and got a bus for Des Moines, where I lived then. He would give me the money, and then shoot himself, that was the plan. But outside of White Sands, New Mexico, he seemed to "come to." He told the driver he wanted to go back to Tucson, and the driver stopped a westbound bus. My father picked up his truck, went back to work. "I still have the gun," he wrote.

And then it was back to flowers and shrubs, his laden grapefruit tree, the sparse new crop of pomegranates.

He's never in his life spoken to me this way, never told me a story in which he seemed so helpless or so open. 1975: year before my mother died, year of the boxes of Miltown, his wife going mad in the back bedroom. Is it the first time he's ever actually said what he felt? It's the first time I've heard him. The gun—the gun he didn't sell after all—has divided all three of us—my father, myself, my mother's ghost—but now it turns in my memory, and manages to bring my old father and me nearer to each other, in closer proximity than we've ever been.

Which is not to say we are not awkward; too late to repair that, but it doesn't matter; I don't expect anything from him. Something between us seems complete.

Which is often the way, I think, with what ruins us: it comes back, to offer us at last—well, nothing we'd have wished for, exactly. Who wouldn't have wanted it all to happen differently! But the thing that harms turns out, sometimes, to be the very thing that restores, the exact thing.

In the autumn of 1997, something happens I'd never have predicted. My father and his second wife come to visit Cape Cod, a day's stop on a bus tour of New England they've taken to see the fall foliage. They have, these years, traveled everywhere together—cruises to Hong Kong and up the Yangtze, up the Pacific Coast to Alaska—and my stepmother's even gotten my father to dancing lessons, and to join a square dance club. The day their group tours the Cape—looking at lighthouses and shopping for souvenirs—Larry and Edith spend with Paul and me.

We've been making ourselves crazy with a ridiculous flurry of preparations; Paul's nervous about meeting them, after all he's heard, and he vacuums as though his life depended on it. We oil the furniture and dust the bookshelves and polish the kitchen till it gleams, or comes as close to gleaming as an old and well-used house, home to two men, two dogs, and two cats, is capable of. I decide the front of the place is looking inexcusably shabby, and two days before Larry and Edith are due to arrive we're up on ladders, wielding scrapers and buckets of paint. From the whirlwind emerge brilliant white clapboards, black shutters, everything redone but the front door, which there's no time for, and anyway we rather like its faded, scaling green, salt-air scoured to just the right patina.

We pick them up at their motel, at the appointed hour, and they chatter away in the backseat about the people in their tour group, and the nice and not-so-great places they've stayed, and the colors of the leaves. They ask Paul questions about himself; I am startled that they seem to find him completely likable. The quality of affection it would perhaps be difficult to direct toward me, complicated as our history is, they offer him unguardedly. He's solicitous of their well-being, and he notices how Edith cares for my father, looking after him, and how he's always careful to make sure things are just as she likes them. We stop at a beachside restaurant—hot dogs and clam chowder, their choice—and when Paul gets up from the table they both say to me, "Such a nice young man."

I say, "He's not *that* young," but they just smile.

When it begins to rain a little and Paul produces a pair of umbrellas from the trunk of the car, my father says, "That Paul thinks of everything."

When we enter the garden gate, the newly painted facade looks bright even in the dim weather. Edith says, "You boys better do something about that front door." The dogs appear, all wiggle and charm—like us, on their best behavior. My father adores them, watching them with a frank, unclouded curiosity I've never seen in his face before. It's as if he's never seen a dog. And then it's as if he's never seen a house like this one. In fact, I guess he hasn't: we tour the little two-hundred-year-old rooms, with their low ceilings and exposed beams, their proudly cracked plaster and odd angles and old furniture.

Edith says, "Well, you boys have a lot of work to do." But my father, who has just been looking all around with that new, unguarded curiosity, says, "Gee, gee." Pause. "This is neat."

We are all a bit shy, a little tentative, and a little startled at how pleasant the visit is. We drive to a favorite beach of mine, Head of the Meadow, a wild strip of high dunes above the Atlantic where the waves break twice, once on a sandbar a ways out to sea, then again as they hurry in to shore. Sand and sky seem immense there, the wide curve endless. It's the last outpost of the continent, nothing but waves between us and Greenland, and the wind always blows in from the rimless expanses chill and fresh, with a tang of the wild.

Edith brings her purse and ties a scarf around her head; my father takes off his shoes and socks and carries them in one hand while we walk the path over a low dune. Paul makes sure they're comfortable walking on the sand; he looks so handsome to me, in his heavy new black sweater, in the shore light. I have the sensation of noticing, all over again, his open and generous face. We step down from the sandhill to the empty slope of shore. My father watches the slap of wave turn to a quick sheet of foam that hurries up the sand and back again, pulled under the dark advancing curve of the next wave, gulls drifting and settling, a racing troop of plovers. He looks simply amazed by it all. I don't think he has any desire to go closer, or to move on, or to do anything just now; his face is full of plain delight.

To tell a story is to take power over it. Now they—we—are part of a tale, a made thing—a perspective box! What begins as a trick of craft makes it possible to stand apart, to—forgive? Not exactly. The stubborn past is not to be dissolved by any act of will, and perhaps we ought at last to be glad for that. What happened defines us, always; erase the darkness in you at your own peril, since it's inextricable at last from who you are.

And who are *you*, anyway—with the shadow you also carry, because you are your parents' son—who are you to forgive? They were nearly helpless, as people are; they did what they knew how to do, under the disfiguring pressure of circumstance. They loved the children whom they brought to harm.

Surely their actions might be something we'd do ourselves: the hand raised to strike could be your hand, the face that trembles to receive the blow your face. The finger on the trigger yours, afraid; the heart held in the gun sights yours also.

And that is close enough to forgiveness, to find that any character in the dream of your life might be you. But you don't know that until you tell the story; caught in the narrative yourself, how could you see from that height?

Though the firebird can; that's the business of birds, to see from the correcting perspective of *above*. All along, the firebird watches, patient in ashes, smoldering till the hour to flame. Just one dance teaches it to believe in the brightness to come. All it ever needed was a practice run, in preparation for someday's full emblazoning.

∾

A visit to Larry and Edith, in Tucson. Historic, for me: at forty-four, I've finally brought my lover home, which ought to be momentous, and is in fact exhausting for us both. It isn't long before even Paul's good spirits flag and wither like some poor unwatered plant in the desert sun.

Larry: "Remember that restaurant you took us to in Provincetown? Well, that sure wasn't four star."

Edith: "Did you boys ever do anything about that front door?"

Larry, later: "Well, Mark, your house sure wouldn't pass the white-glove test."

And so the sniping continues; we sit at the kitchen table and talk and when that fails—after I lose my temper with my father, who has suggested I might get a job in the casino industry, if the college professor thing doesn't pan out—we look for things to do. We drive out to the Desert Museum, in the foothills outside of town, a beautiful place where the plants and wildlife of Sonora are displayed along long looping trails, in habitats artfully contrived to look like the real thing—a rocky cliff for bighorn sheep, a den for mountain lions, a huge scrubby enclosure for the javelinas, one of which, Edith informs us, once bit her on the butt. Larry and Edith walk more slowly than Paul and I, and fall behind, and when we come to a fork in the path I can't stop myself; I pull him in the rougher, less-traveled direction, heading off into the scrub where I know my parents won't go, and I take a deep, childish pleasure in walking with him in the sun far out of the reach of their conversation, and I make sure we look at every single display.

And so my parents and I make it clear, over the course of a weekend, that reconciliation and resolution are things that happen in stories, and are never complete in this life.

∾

In spring the Virgin Mary appeared in Salt Lake City, on a stormy night in the barrio near downtown—only seven blocks, really, from the Mormon Temple, but a world away. A man was waiting for a bus at the edge of a small city park, a strip of bricked playground and large trees. I've heard two versions: either there was a crack of lightning, which caused a limb to fall, or the lightning caused the man to turn, beneath his umbrella, to see what was illuminated in the scar where a long-ago limb had fallen or been cut away.

Centered in the circle of the tree's wound was the silhouette of the Virgin of Guadalupe, slick with rain. Because the man at the bus stop was devout, he first prayed and then ran to fetch someone else to see it. News of the apparition began to travel through the neighborhood before the thunder even stopped.

When the storm was over, the Virgincita remained as shiny as she had been before, when she'd gleamed with what had seemed to be rainwater. Now it became apparent that what poured from the image were her tears, which came both from her eyes and from the region of her heart. Through the night, and all the next day, and then through the days thereafter, the apparition in the tree was attended by the faithful, and her weeping did not cease.

There wasn't any story in the papers; I heard about "the Vision," as everyone called it, from my students. I'd come to Salt Lake to teach at the University of Utah, and it was late in the semester, in May, when some of the graduate poets told us the story, and that they'd been to see the vision at the corner of First and Seventh. Paul and I drove there as soon as we could.

It was easy to find. The holy tree was right beside the sidewalk, and the police had cordoned off a portion of the street with wooden barriers, to allow the crowd at park's edge to spill over the curb and onto the asphalt. A line of people coiled along the walk, waiting their turn to climb a portable metal ladder wheeled into place beside the trunk, which was entirely encrusted with rosaries and paper flowers and *milagros*, and dozens of photographs: snapshots of parents who'd died, of soldiers, of sick children, pictures of babies with handwritten prayers penned on folded pieces of paper tacked beside them. The tree seemed dressed, wrapped in glory and supplication.

I loved watching the people in line: homeboys in big jackets and oversize jeans, couples with children in their arms and in strollers, little kids by themselves, teenage girls with elaborately heaped and sprayed hair. Two *viejas* with megaphones sat beside the trunk in folding chairs; *maestras*, they kept watch, shepherded the pilgrims up and down the ladder, and led the rosary, even while they offered instruction or kept everyone in line, their prayer somehow uninterrupted: *Hail Mary*, in Spanish, again and again, a dry soft drone which became that evening's music.

It was nearly dark, and shadowy around the edges of the park, where more people gathered, ate ice creams, and talked softly or watched the people coming and going, but every face near the tree was lit by the glow of a huge bank of candles beneath the trunk, the wavering glow of each individual flame made steady by the great number of them. The light cast by the sum of all those votives, in their clear or blue glass holders, their red jars engraved with images of Guadalupe, was steady and warm.

It wasn't my church, so I didn't feel I could climb the ladder myself, though perhaps I should have. I watched as each mounted up, and crossed herself, and touched fingers to the tears. Some rubbed them on their foreheads; others crossed themselves again with the holy stuff; one woman touched a handkerchief to the wood, soaking up a bit of the precious fluid in order to carry it home with her, or to bring it to someone. One man kissed the image. Each person looked at it gravely; the entire procession, in fact, was solemn and earnest, without irony, and beautiful in that it was unmediated, uninterpreted, without clergy or hierarchy, merely the two old women softly directing the movement of traffic while they told their beads.

Why am I telling you this?

How can I say what I felt for that weeping mother? I hear they've now covered her image in Plexiglas, for protection, and that her tears collect in a dish beneath her, into which the faithful dip their fingers and rosaries. The trunk below the wound has entirely disappeared beneath its freight of prayer and ornament. I love the democracy of the visionary; each person in that line, carrying distinct sorrows like or unlike in scale and nature, finds hope there. Our Mother of Sorrows subsumes all individual griefs. She does not care what the sorrow is; it isn't the Mother's to judge or to differentiate or to explain; it's the Mother's work to love and therefore to weep for us, to enfold us in her weeping.

It is Her role to stand, where a mother once stood, as our Mother. The human failings—the ordinary desires and limits and lacks—of our real mothers brought them and us to harm, made them incapable of embodying their love for their children as they might have wished to. In this Mother there is no such failing. My mother prayed to the Mother of Sorrows because she could not be that Mother herself, filled as she was with rage and her longing for some other life, with her dislike and distrust of the body and her disappointment in her own children.

You don't need to be Catholic to love Mary, or even a Christian; I have little traffic with her Son, but the Holy Mother is another story. Through her, through the image emblazoned on the tree and pouring herself out for us, I can come close to—how else to say it?—that maternal wellspring deep in the heart of the world. She is permanent affection; she sits on a donkey with her body bent over her baby and carries him into Egypt, out of danger. She's pharaoh's daughter, who bends over the Nile reeds to pluck the basket from the eddies, to bring the babe to the warm light and laughter of her chambers.

And how then could it matter anymore, that what flowed to me individually from my mother was poisoned, finally, tainted with bitterness? Human love is always imperfect, carries within it some degree or other of darkness; our mothers nurse us with an inevitable blend of milk and shadow, the source both of our love and our estrangement.

But not tonight; no strangers here. Every one of us—all these Latino men and women, and their children, and the boys in their hip clothes, and the white policemen, and the curious grad students, the ice cream vendor and the happy *viejas*, and even Paul and I, two white gay boys with our short hair and outfits out of sync with the neighborhood—we all belong here, since we are her beloved children, bathed in candlelight and the headlights of passing cars, waiting our turn to be cleansed by her tears.

Acknowledgments

The allegiance of this book is to memory; this is a past colored, arranged, and choreographed entirely by that transforming, idiosyncratic light. Any character here might well see things entirely differently. As my sister—bless her—put it, "Well, the things you got wrong just make it that much more *you*." I'm more grateful to her than I can say, for her forbearance, for her understanding and acceptance of what can't always have been easy.

My gratitude, too, to a band of readers—Michael Carter, Bernard Cooper, Martha Christina, Elizabeth McCracken, Carol Muske, and Maggie Valentine—who read this book in many of its incarnations, and offered good advice and great company.

Bill Clegg read with acute insight, and then represented the book with such heroic energy and professionalism that I'm permanently in his debt. Robert Jones, as ever, proved the most devoted, perceptive, and hardworking editor luck could bring me; he offers every day the kind of association writers mostly just dream about.

Paul Lisicky heard every one of these pages, in their raw new form, then read every word over and over again, so that the language seems something shared, as well as the memories that language evokes. In this way it is his book almost as much as it is my own.

∾

And to the Virgin of Guadalupe: thank you.

200

M
a
r
k

D
o
t
y

 Perennial

Books by Mark Doty:

FIREBIRD

ISBN 0-06-093497-3 (paperback)

In this powerful memoir, Doty shapes a radiant study of growing up
gay amidst his family's dissolution through the corrosive power of
alcohol, sorrow, and desire. It is also a wry evocation of childhood
pleasures and terrors, and a comic tour of suburban American life in
the 50s and 60s, which is both lyrical and shattering.

**"[A] beautifully written, hallucinatory evocative memoir of growing up
gay in baby-boom America. Four stars."** — *Newsweek*

HEAVEN'S COAST

ISBN 0-06-092805-0 (paperback)

Part memoir, part elegy for a life of rare communication and beauty,
Heaven's Coast recalls the journey of Doty's partner's struggle with
terminal illness.

**"In sharing his own pain and love, Doty offers a kind of survivor's guide,
not just to those who have lost a lover to AIDS, but to anyone who is, after
all, only human."** — *San Francisco Chronicle*

ATLANTIS

ISBN 0-06-095106-0 (paperback)

A collection of poems which seek to reconcile with, and even to cele-
brate, the evanescence of our earthy connections, and to understand how
we can love more at the very moment that we must consent to let go.

**"Mark Doty has written a book that is ferocious, luminous, and
important."** — *Mary Oliver*

SWEET MACHINE

ISBN 0-06-095256-3 (paperback)

A collection of poems which view the world from a new perspective—
a coming back to life, after so much death, a way of seeing the body's
"sweet machine not simply as a time bomb, but also as a vibrant,
sensual, living thing.

"Moving, splendidly observant and unflinching."
— Citation for the Writer *Bynner Prize for Poetry* awarded by the
American Academy of Arts and Letters

Available wherever books are sold, or call 1-800-331-3761 to order.